LIVING SIMPLY

A TEEN GUIDE TO MINIMALISM

SALLY McGRAW

TWENTY-FIRST CENTURY BOOKS / MINNEAPOLIS

Twenty-First Century Books
A division of Lerner Publishing Group, Inc.
241 First Avenue North
Minneapolis, MN 55401 USA

For reading levels and more information, look up this title at www.lernerbooks.com.

Main body text set in Adrianna Regular 11/15.
Typeface provided by Chank.

Library of Congress Cataloging-in-Publication Data

The Cataloging-in-Publication Data for *Living Simply: A Teen Guide to Minimalism* is on file at the Library of Congress.
ISBN 978-1-5415-0054-9 (lib. bdg.)
ISBN 978-1-5415-2482-8 (eb pdf)

Manufactured in the United States of America
1-43697-33489-6/7/2018

CONTENTS

Teen girls pedal along the Shining Sea Bikeway in Falmouth, Massachusetts. Minimalism involves making Earth-friendly choices, such as biking instead of traveling by car.

INTRODUCTION
MINIMALISM MATTERS

Minimalism matters because you matter. Since you're reading this book, you're concerned about our planet. You're especially concerned about waste. You probably turn off the water while you're brushing your teeth, recycle faithfully, and bike or walk everywhere you can. You might even be able to reel off a few staggering stats, such as these about how human waste is slowly suffocating our planet:

- Every year humans create 1.3 billion tons (1.2 billion t) of solid waste, better known as garbage. Experts expect that number to soar to 4 billion tons (3.6 billion t) by 2100.

- About 50 percent of all fresh fruits and veggies in the United States are thrown away uneaten. That's about 60 million tons (54 million t) of produce every year.
- Americans discard 14 million tons (13 million t) of clothing every year. While a portion of that clothing goes to resale charities such as Goodwill and the Salvation Army, much of it goes into landfills.

That's so much stuff that could've been recycled or reused, and so many items that should never have been bought. We're burying ourselves in garbage and buying new things when our old stuff is actually just fine.

The good news is that many people are looking for ways to become more responsible, low-impact citizens of Earth. If a purchase or choice isn't ethical, recyclable, organic, or environmentally friendly, many of us give it some serious side-eye. Our collective willingness to step up and make smart, informed, impactful choices about what we buy, what we eat, and how we use energy are crucial steps in saving our planet.

KEEP IT SIMPLE

Minimalism is a lifestyle that involves using less, minimizing harm to the environment, and owning only useful items. The philosophy focuses on the things we most value and letting go of everything that distracts us from that focus.

For some people, minimalism means living with less. For residents of this community of tiny homes in Madison, Wisconsin, that involves paring down possessions to whatever fits in just 98 square feet (9.1 sq. m).

It isn't a new philosophy, but in the twenty-first century, it's gone mainstream. Authors, bloggers, and podcasters all over the world have adopted the minimalist living cause and are helping others learn how to live with less. Books about decluttering are runaway international best sellers, and minimalist bloggers such as Joshua Becker have millions of followers. The tiny house movement, which challenges individuals to live in just a few hundred square feet or less of space, has swept the United States. Some organizations focus their minimalism efforts on reducing waste. For instance, the clothing brands Eileen Fisher and H&M have created garment-recycling programs to cut down on the amount of clothing sent to landfills. Feeding the 5000, a United Kingdom–based charity, sponsors huge events where perfectly edible but misshapen or blemished grocery store castoffs are cooked and eaten.

When you embrace minimalism, your choices and actions can be influential. For example, when you pare down your wardrobe and other possessions, your friends and peers see that for you, flaunting new stuff isn't the only way to be cool. Younger siblings may be inspired to follow your lead and use their own money more wisely. You may have some great conversations with your parents about how spending habits matter. The ways in which you do and don't spend your hard-earned cash have an effect on virtually everyone around you.

If you'd like to increase that impact, your nose is buried in the right book. This is a hands-on guide to reducing waste, buying less, and making good use of what you already have. We'll talk fashion, food, and living spaces, offering suggestions for meeting your needs and fulfilling your desires in Earth-friendly ways. We'll explore the difference between decluttering and true minimalist living. We'll even meet teens who absolutely adore shopping, spending, and indulging who are living with less. We'll dig into simple and effective ways to live a stylish, modern, compassionate life without leaving a giant, wasteful footprint on Earth.

In earlier eras, humans often grew their own food and made their own clothing. In this advertisement from 1851, a woman makes clothing using a foot-powered sewing machine.

CHAPTER 1

THE ROOTS OF MINIMALISM

Did you know that our earliest ancestors were thrifters and that they made just about everything they needed from scratch? The earliest humans were hunter-gatherers. They lived in small groups and moved from place to place, hunting animals and gathering wild plants for food. Hunter-gatherers fashioned tools from animal bones, rocks, and wood; made clothing from animal hides; and built shelters out of wood, clay, straw, animal skins, and other natural materials. If a tool broke or an item of clothing ripped, the owner repaired it with twine or thread made from plant fibers.

The first farmers on Earth lived about twelve thousand

years ago in the ancient Middle East. Early farming was Earth-friendly. Families grew and processed enough food to feed themselves. If they had any surplus, they stored it or traded it. Livestock grazed on plants, and farmers used the animals' dung to fertilize crops.

Cities developed shortly after the start of farming. People built almost everything in early cities, from roads and bridges to houses and government buildings, by hand with mostly local materials. City dwellers either made their own tools, clothes, and furniture or purchased them from local artisans. They patched and repaired most items as needed. If someone did throw an item away, the materials—wood, animal hides, plant fibers, or other once-living tissues— eventually broke down and enriched the soil. Human trash benefited the planet in those days.

THE RISE OF CONSUMER CULTURE

The Industrial Revolution began in England in the late eighteenth century and soon spread to the rest of Europe and North America. For the first time, manufacturers used engines powered by steam (and later coal and petroleum) to run machinery. They hired workers for factories, where items were mass-produced. Most city dwellers also made goods by hand or bought them from craftspeople, but factories began to mass-produce clothing, tools, and other items.

When industrialization began, most Americans were thrifty. They conserved and reused everything they could.

By the 1920s, US consumers could choose from hundreds of canned and boxed food products. Stores also offered a vast array of factory-made clothing, toiletries, cosmetics, and home appliances.

Factory-made items were alluring but expensive, so most people continued to use and reuse what they already had. People sold their worn or unrepairable broken items. In big US cities, recyclers called rag-and-bone men went door-to-door, buying scrap paper, metal, cloth, and even animal bones left over from meals. The rag-and-bone men sold the scraps to businesses that recycled them. For instance, some businesses melted down scrap metal and fashioned it into new tools or containers. Papermakers shredded old cloth, mixed it with water, mashed it into a pulp, and formed it into sheets of paper. Other businesses ground up old animal bones and sold them to farmers for fertilizer.

Over time, with innovations such as the assembly line, mass-produced products became much more affordable.

By the early 1920s, even working-class families could afford newly invented cars, radios, vacuum cleaners, and other items. Consumer culture was off and running through aggressive advertising that encouraged consumers to buy. Low prices and the ability to buy on credit tempted them further. Store-bought clothes and canned foods became more popular than homemade varieties. In this era, many US cities set up trash-removal services for the first time. Residents tossed old newspapers, empty cans and bottles, broken appliances, and other unwanted materials into garbage cans. City workers hauled the trash to landfills and giant incinerators. Americans began to throw away more and reuse less.

ENFORCED CONSERVATION

In 1929 the US stock market crashed, leading to the Great Depression (1929–1942). This worldwide economic downturn ended when the United States entered World War II (1939–1945). During the Depression, businesses and banks went broke, and millions of people lost their jobs and couldn't find work. In the United States, poverty forced many into a severely minimalist life. Families cut back on everything from clothing to food. They became hyperaware of abundance and waste, worrying whether they'd have enough food to eat or enough money to pay the rent. Many Americans had to ensure that everyday items, such as a single pair of pants or shoes, would last for many years. They repaired and mended because they couldn't afford to buy new. The situation was so dire that the US government set up a variety of programs to employ Americans, assist farmers, and regulate business practices to prevent future economic disasters.

World War II brought more years of scarcity. The US government wanted to ensure that its soldiers had enough food and clothing and that its armies fighting in Europe and Asia had enough weapons, ammunition, vehicles, and fuel. The government set up a program of rationing. Each civilian household could buy only small amounts of gasoline, butter, sugar, coal, firewood, and even shoes. That way, the military wouldn't run short of key materials. To make the most of every drop, shred, and shard, the government encouraged Americans to collect scrap metal, paper, and rubber. Through community scrap drives, Americans donated millions of pounds of materials. The scrap metal was recycled into weapons. Scrap rubber became tires for tanks and other military vehicles. Americans even donated old cooking grease to make explosives. The country became mindful of waste and focused on recycling.

NEW MATERIALS, NEW HABITS

After the war, the US economy boomed. Instead of producing military goods, factories began to churn out new foods, clothes, cars, and household appliances. Consumer goods were plentiful—and cheap. One big reason was plastic. Made from petroleum, plastics were developed in the early twentieth century. During World War II,

This sign from the Philadelphia Council of Defense encouraged city residents to donate scrap metal, paper, rubber, and other materials to assist the military in World War II. Recyclers turned the donated scrap into weapons and other gear for soldiers.

engineers used plastic to make insulation, tires, and other parts for military vehicles. After the war, manufacturers used plastic to make everything from toys and dishes to lawn furniture and telephones. Manufacturers also used petroleum to make paints, adhesives, solvents, and synthetic (human-made) fibers.

THE ROOTS OF MINIMALISM

Plastic is cheap, strong, and lightweight. Manufacturers can form it into millions of different products. Synthetic fibers, such as nylon and polyester, are also strong and inexpensive to produce. But over time, these substances do not break down into harmless or beneficial particles the way natural materials do. They can take hundreds of years to break down into tiny bits of plastic, and they release toxic chemicals.

In the 1950s and 1960s, plastics and synthetics were new and exciting. They were everywhere. Eager to make their own lives easier, simpler, and cleaner, people happily traded reusable goods for disposable ones. Why wash filthy cloth diapers when you could buy plastic-lined diapers and pitch them into the trash after one use? Why do the dishes after a party when you could use plastic plates, cups, and flatware and toss them out? Advertising for plastics and other innovations encouraged a wasteful lifestyle.

Plastic revolutionized the American kitchen after World War II. One of the most popular product lines was Tupperware. Consumers loved the unbreakable, resealable plastic containers, which could be used for both storing and serving food.

Americans who had lived through the enforced minimalist years of the 1930s and 1940s became happy maximalists. Many spent money on new stuff as fast as they could, throwing things away quickly and loving every minute of it.

Also after World War II, the United States was in the middle of a dire housing shortage. Many young families were crowded into the homes of relatives and friends. To provide much-needed housing, real estate developers began converting farmland into suburban neighborhoods. Consumers rapidly and eagerly purchased the new homes. Many suburban residents had to commute long distances to get to their downtown jobs. Yet most municipalities didn't expand their public transit systems to accommodate these commuters. So suburban families became increasingly dependent on their cars. Cars that run on gasoline emit carbon monoxide, hydrocarbons, nitrogen oxides, and other pollutants through their exhaust pipes. Without realizing the long-term impact of car culture, Americans were shifting toward a lifestyle that generated large amounts of trash and spewed pollution into the air.

WAKING UP TO WASTE

In the 1960s, many Americans began to question business as usual in the United States. It was a decade of great political and cultural change. African Americans fought for their civil rights, women fought for equality with men, and gays and lesbians proudly began to proclaim their identities.

ANIMAL, VEGETABLE, MINIMAL

The modern minimalist movement concerns itself primarily with food, clothing, and other consumer products. But minimalist movements also have swept through art, architecture, and even music.

Art used to be showy. For instance, in the seventeenth century, baroque art and architecture were all the rage across Europe. Baroque paintings featured ornate gold frames and detailed scenes with dozens of figures: people, horses, angels, and more. Baroque buildings were over-the-top dramatic, with high ceilings, curving walls, and sculptural adornments. Later artistic styles were simpler but still boasted an array of color, clutter, and intricate detail.

All that changed in the early twentieth century. First came a movement called De Stijl (which means "the style" in Dutch). It focused on clarity, order, simple geometric forms, and primary colors. Dutch painter Piet Mondrian, the movement's most famous artist, created bold canvases filled with crisp lines and stark shapes.

In Germany in the 1920s and early 1930s, a school called the Bauhaus trained industrial designers, graphic designers, interior designers, and architects. Similar to artists of De Stijl, students of the Bauhaus created simple, unadorned works. Bauhaus architects designed boxy, austere buildings. Bauhaus furniture designers made clean-lined (but often uncomfortable) chairs.

Fast-forward to the late 1960s. A group of artists in New York City wanted to push society to wonder what made something art. Among the first artists to call themselves minimalists, they created giant cubes of steel, black aluminum X shapes, black-on-black painted canvases, and other spare works. This group included the US painters Frank Stella and

Ellsworth Kelly and US sculptors Tony Smith and Sol LeWitt. The minimalist movement in art led to similar approaches in product design, advertising, typography, and magazine layouts of the late twentieth century.

Also, late in the century, critics applied the word *minimalist* to the works of writers, including US short story master Raymond Carver and Irish playwright Samuel Beckett. Their minimalist writings were short, stripped down, and light on detail. Minimalist musical works, created by composers such as the Americans John Cage and Philip Glass, featured short, repeated patterns of sound and even long silences.

One might think of minimalist movements in art, writing, and music as simply cultural trends. But minimalism in the arts often stems from deeper social ideals. Many minimalists want to challenge established ideas about art, to provide a stark contrast to the complexities of modern society, and to ask audiences to consider the value of simplicity.

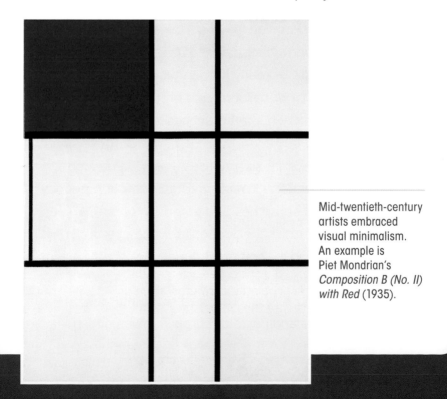

Mid-twentieth-century artists embraced visual minimalism. An example is Piet Mondrian's *Composition B (No. II) with Red* (1935).

Young people protested against US involvement in the Vietnam War (1957–1975). And many Americans woke up to the damage that humans were inflicting on the environment. US biologist Rachel Carson helped launch the environmental protection movement with her 1962 book *Silent Spring*. Carson shed light on the dangers of pesticides. Farmers use these chemicals to kill insects that feed on crops. Pesticides help farmers grow more crops, but the chemicals can also pollute soil, groundwater, and water ways. Carson reported that dichloro-diphenyl-trichloroethane (DDT), a widely used pesticide that killed a variety of insects, was particularly harmful. When birds and other animals ate the poisoned bugs, they were poisoned. DDT caused some birds to lay eggs with extremely thin shells. The shells broke before healthy baby birds could be born. Populations of pelicans, eagles, and other birds declined. Carson's book opened Americans' eyes to the harmful ripple effects of many human technologies.

As more evidence of polluting and other harmful consequences of many human practices appeared, Americans became outraged. Eventually, the US government stepped in to regulate these practices. In 1970 President Richard Nixon created the Environmental Protection Agency (EPA). This agency establishes and enforces rules that keep air and water pollution in check, regulates the use of harmful pesticides, and prohibits the use of dangerous chemicals in common household items.

In the 1980s and 1990s, organized recycling took off in the United States and parts of Europe. Towns and cities

Planet Earth is drowning in trash. People bury it in landfills, burn it in giant incinerators, and sometimes just dump it outside. Rather than trashing items you don't need, considering recycling, donating, or upcycling them.

began building recycling plants and setting up curbside recycling programs. The goal was to reduce the amount of trash heading into landfills and incinerators. The efforts were effective. In 2012 the EPA reported that Americans were recycling 34.5 percent of their household waste.

Yet even though some people recycle faithfully, the twenty-first-century world is still drowning in trash. The EPA estimates that Americans generated 88 million tons (80 million t) of garbage in 1960. By 2015 that number had almost tripled, to 254 million tons (230 million t) annually. On a global scale, the statistics are even more alarming. In 2015 the World Bank (an international agency that offers financial assistance to poor nations) reported that people across the globe were creating 1.3 billion tons (1.2 billion t) of solid waste a year and that volume was expected to increase to 2.2 billion tons (2 billion t) by 2025.

THE ROOTS OF MINIMALISM

LIFE ON A COMMUNE

The commune movement of the 1960s is one example of the minimalist movement in the United States. Communal living had been a countercultural tradition for hundreds of years, with the earliest American communes recorded in 1663. But the 1960s saw a strong resurgence in interest in this alternative lifestyle. Then many young people (often called hippies) embraced the counterculture. This philosophy of living rejected consumerism and mainstream values in

In the 1960s and 1970s, many young people embraced minimalism by joining communes. Here, two residents tend a garden at a commune in Wales in the 1970s.

favor of a more Earth-friendly lifestyle. Some members of the counterculture dropped out of college, rejected suburban life, and shunned office jobs. Instead, they moved to multifamily communities known as communes.

Communes broke with traditional social norms. People in a commune pitched in to keep the shared community clean and working smoothly. They shared duties and work according to skills rather than gender or education. Many communes were in rural areas, where residents grew their own organic food. Members tried to have relatively little impact on the environment. They set up alternative energy such as solar and wind power. They repaired and reused as much as they could to minimize waste. Communes were minimalist havens.

Taylor Camp in Hawaii was just one of hundreds of communes that operated in the United States in the late 1960s and early 1970s. Thirteen hippies established the camp in 1969 on a 7-acre (2.8 ha) plot of land (donated to them by Howard Taylor, the brother of famous actor Elizabeth Taylor) on the island of Kauai. The commune thrived for five years, boasting more than one hundred residents at its peak. Taylor Camp residents used found materials to build treehouse homes. They grew crops, gathered wild foods from the surrounding land, and accepted donations of food from neighbors and friends. The entire community shared all the food. Residents established unwritten laws and chose a mayor and a sheriff. In the warm Hawaiian sunshine, many residents were nudists. They took minimalism to the extreme by deciding that clothing was unnecessary.

Communes are difficult to maintain over a long period, and the counterculture commune movement of the 1960s eventually faded away. But many of the ideals live on in the modern minimalist movement.

In the United States, most garbage ends up in landfills or incinerators. These facilities must operate according to rules and regulations designed to minimize pollution of the soil, air, and water. But many poorer nations don't have curbside trash collection or regulated facilities for trash disposal. More than half the world's population lacks access to regular trash collection services. In many places, people dump trash along roadsides and into rivers.

GLOBAL REPERCUSSIONS

Garbage is one problem, but let's talk about another— greenhouse gases. These gases—mainly carbon dioxide, methane, and nitrous oxide—trap the sun's heat in Earth's atmosphere. By burning fossil fuels (coal, petroleum, and natural gas), humans add about 44 billion tons (40 billion t) of carbon dioxide into the air each year. Most cars, trucks, and farm vehicles run on gasoline, which comes from petroleum. Many factories burn coal to operate their machinery. Many people heat their homes and businesses by burning natural gas. Burning solid waste (trash) in incinerators also adds greenhouse gases to the atmosphere.

Because of the volume of heat-trapping gases in the air, temperatures on Earth are rising. The warmer air, soil, and oceans are changing climates (weather patterns) around the world. Hurricanes and other storms are becoming more powerful, droughts (periods of little or no rainfall) are increasing, and heat waves are lasting longer.

NO-CHOICE MINIMALISM

Twenty-first-century minimalist philosophy is a product of wealthy, industrialized cultures. Americans and residents of other rich nations are drowning in stuff—and the minimalist movement is a reaction to this excess. But around the world, billions of people don't have to change behaviors to become minimalists. Many live in modest homes with very few belongings because they simply cannot afford more or better things.

In many parts of the world, minimalism is the only possible way of living. People must grow their own food, make their own clothing, and reuse absolutely everything because they cannot afford or they do not have access to store-bought goods. American writer and human rights activist Jacquelene Adam has lived in the African nation of Ghana. She describes the many commonplace Earth-friendly practices among her neighbors in the city of Accra. They conserve precious water by bathing with just one 5-gallon (19 L) bucket split between two people. In the town's frequent blackouts—periods when the electricity fails—they rely on candles and battery-powered lights. They wash and dry clothing and dishes by hand. They are extremely careful to put every scrap of food to good use.

Adams' neighbors in Ghana did not choose to be minimalists. Living in poverty forced them to conserve and make do. Minimalism can be fulfilling and challenging to those in wealthy nations—those who have many choices about what they eat and consume. For those in poor nations, living with less can be a struggle for survival.

Warmer temperatures on Earth are creating more extreme weather, such as killer storms and floods. In this photo from June 2017, bicycles and buses struggle to move through flooded streets in Dhaka, Bangladesh.

The higher temperatures are even melting ice at the North Pole and South Pole. As the ice melts into the oceans, sea levels rise, flooding coastal cities and island nations.

Climate change has far-reaching impacts on both humans and animals. Changes in rainfall and snowfall affect the availability and quantity of drinkable water. Natural disasters such as hurricanes and floods destroy housing and farmland. In oceans, lakes, and rivers, the combination of warmer water, excess carbon, and water pollution is killing off coral reefs, aquatic plants, fish, and sea mammals.

WHAT CAN BE DONE?

Efforts are under way to reduce carbon emissions. Around the world, businesses, governments, and homeowners are slowly switching from fossil fuels to nonpolluting energy sources, such as solar and wind power. Manufacturers are selling electric cars, which don't release toxic emissions. The organic farming movement—growing crops without chemical pesticides and fertilizers—is booming. More consumers are becoming locavores—eating foods produced locally and requiring minimal transportation to get to market.

The minimalist movement is a big part of the effort to tread more lightly on Earth. The movement marks an important shift in thinking. It shows that after decades of wasteful consumption, many people are eager to change and to protect the future of the planet.

By spending their money on Earth-friendly clothing, food, and household items, teens can make a powerful positive impact.

CHAPTER 2

MAKING MINIMALIST CHOICES

Nearly twenty-eight million teens live in the United States, and those who hold jobs collectively rake in $91.1 billion every year. Since many of you don't have to pay for rent or groceries, much of that $91.1 billion is spendable. As a group, you and your peers are among the most important consumers in the nation—possibly the world, since the United States is one of the most powerful economic forces on the planet. But as the saying goes, with great power comes great responsibility.

How you choose to spend your chunk of that $91.1 billion can have a huge impact on the global economy. Corporations are watching you and tracking your shopping patterns. When you shop online, retailers, marketing companies, and data aggregators track your searches, preferences, and purchases using cookies, or pieces of computer code that record user activity. Businesses also monitor your "likes" and purchases through code embedded in social media. So every time you buy lip balm made with organic oils and plants or buy a solar-powered phone charger, you're sending a message. You're voting with your dollars. You're telling corporations that you want and value stuff that doesn't damage Earth. You're encouraging them to use environmentally friendly farming and manufacturing practices.

To send this message, shoppers have to make mindful, or thoughtful, decisions. But this can be challenging in a world that's constantly shoving new, fun, cheap goodies under our noses and when we see our classmates indulge in nonstop shopping. Advertising surrounds us and follows us as we watch TV, cruise the internet, and rock out to the radio. The messages we hear about buying and spending linger in your mind and influence behavior.

Mindful consumption isn't always easy. But when we use our dollars to vote for Earth-friendly products, when we buy fewer things overall, and when we opt to live simply, we're helping nudge our world toward a brighter future.

FAST FASHION IS TRASHING THE WORLD

Buying five-dollar tees and fifteen-dollar jeans at H&M is undeniably enjoyable. Snagging an entirely new back-to-school

MEET A YOUNG MINIMALIST: OWEN RADER

Owen, fourteen, is a minimalist. He had already embraced the philosophy and lifestyle by the age of thirteen. Here are some of his thoughts about minimalism:

Why do you consider yourself a minimalist?

I try and limit the things I own mostly to keep things simple and easy to access. For example, I wouldn't have to sift through an ocean of desk toys and device chargers to find my pen. I think when it comes to minimalism, you have to be organized too, not just not have a lot of stuff.

What are some of the ways you try to live with less on a daily basis?

On a daily basis . . . I don't think too much about it. In my opinion, I've gotten to a place where I'm pretty happy about how much stuff I have.

What's hardest about living this way?

The hardest part about living like this is probably having to decide between what is important to you out of a whole lot of stuff that you've had for years and which all seems important to you.

What's fun, rewarding, or awesome about living this way?

It's really rewarding to just not have a lot of stuff. When you've got a whole bunch of useless stuff that you don't ever use, and it occupies the same space as you do, you almost feel like a prisoner. And it's just great to be free.

What advice would you give to someone who wants to have a smaller impact on Earth but isn't sure where to start?

Start small. You'll find you have a lot of tiny little things that you forgot you had, and removing those makes a big difference. Once you get going, it's as easy as pie!

wardrobe at JCPenney for under $200 is exhilarating. But you might not know that the economic forces that make those tees and jeans so affordable are destructive in multiple, mind-blowing ways.

Fast fashion is a trend within the clothing industry that involves getting inexpensive versions of new styles onto retail racks as quickly as possible. Spanish clothing giant Zara has perfected the art of fast fashion. The company often ensures that new clothing is designed, manufactured, and in stores in just five weeks. The quicker a clothing brand can get its goods into your hands, the more money it can make. That means factories that produce the clothing must also operate at lightning speed. That's where the trouble with fast fashion starts.

Fast fashion impacts the environment. Fashion is the second-dirtiest industry on Earth. Only the petroleum industry creates more pollution. Clothing factories are responsible for 10 percent of all global carbon emissions.

Look at the neck tags on your favorite garments. These tags tell you what materials the clothing is made from. Are your clothes mostly made of acrylic, nylon, or polyester? These are synthetic fabrics, made from petroleum. Producing synthetic materials releases huge amounts of polluting chemicals into the air and water. This production also releases 1.5 trillion pounds (680 billion kg) of greenhouse gases into the atmosphere every year. That's the equivalent of the annual emissions of 185 coal-fired power plants. Synthetics manufacturing is dirty business—no two ways about it. But even producing fabrics out of natural fibers, such

More than one thousand workers died when this building collapsed in Bangladesh in 2013. The poorly built structure housed garment factories, where workers toiled for long hours and barebones pay to make inexpensive clothing for US retailers.

as cotton, uses vast amounts of resources. Consider that it takes 713 gallons (2,699 L) of water—about what one person drinks in two and a half years—to make a cotton shirt.

Fast fashion impacts the people who make the clothes. In April 2013, an eight-story building in Dhaka, Bangladesh, collapsed. The structure had been built quickly and cheaply. Its upper floors held heavy power generators that shook the building when they operated. The shaking cracked the structure's concrete beams and pillars, which eventually crumbled to the ground. The building housed clothing factories that produced items for big American retailers, including Walmart. When the structure gave way, it killed more than 1,110 factory workers. Also in Bangladesh, a fire in a clothing factory killed 112 workers in November 2012. Unsafe working conditions in a clothing factory have claimed other workers' lives.

The harmful cycle goes something like this: Big-name clothing brands want their items produced quickly and cheaply. They ask several factories, usually based in poor nations, to bid on the job. The factory that offers to produce the goods at the lowest cost and in the shortest amount of time gets the contract. These factories are already operating quickly. To speed up production even more, factory owners push their workers harder. They might ask employees to work eighteen hours per day or even longer. The factory owners don't spend money on sound building construction or fire safety. They don't make sure that the air inside factories is clean and free of chemicals. They don't pay their workers a fair, living wage. In Bangladesh, for example, the daily wage of a garment industry worker is only about $1.20.

Fast fashion impacts waste production. Americans discard 14 million tons (13 million t) of clothing every year, which breaks down to about 80 pounds (36 kg) per person. Almost all that clothing could be recycled, but most of it ends up in landfills instead. Clothing made from synthetic fibers can take hundreds of years to break down in a landfill. It breaks down into harmful substances—into tinier and tinier synthetic pieces. And it releases toxic gases.

It may seem as if a pair of jeans or a plastic necklace here and there won't make a huge difference. But multiplied by millions of consumers over days, weeks, months, and years, those occasional purchases add up. Are you still tempted by that five-dollar H&M polyester tee?

YOU ARE HOW YOU EAT

If your home has a pantry packed with snacks and a fridge brimming with fresh fruits and veggies, you're very fortunate. It's easy to forget that many people on Earth don't have access to supermarkets filled with a wide variety of affordable foods. It's easy to forget that in poor nations, many people go hungry or starve. Even in the United States, the richest nation on Earth, more than 12 percent of households are food insecure—meaning that families don't have regular access to affordable and nutritious food.

Let's ponder a second layer of food privilege: waste. An American family of four typically throws away $1,600 worth of produce every year. That's just fruit and veggies! The US Department of Agriculture, a federal government agency, estimates that US residents throw away between 30 and 40 percent of the food they buy.

Americans excel at pitching out food, including massive amounts of tasty consumables that are in no way rotten or inedible. Much food waste begins on the farm. Believing that US consumers don't want misshapen, bruised, or discolored produce, farmers sometimes throw away this produce right after it's harvested—even though it's perfectly safe and nutritious. They may even leave it in the fields to rot. Manufacturers put sell by, use by, and best before dates on grocery items to show when the food is at its peak quality. Many shoppers and retailers throw food away when the listed date has passed. Yet most foods are safe to eat days, weeks, and even months afterward. In restaurants, diners

Grocery stores often throw out nutritious produce just because it's bruised or blemished. Farms, restaurants, and households also throw away perfectly edible food. Minimalists are mindful of food waste. They buy only what they need, eat what they buy, and use any scraps to make compost.

leave uneaten food on plates and kitchen staff toss out unsold meals and unused ingredients. According to the EPA, 15 percent of all the food that ends up in landfills comes from restaurants.

The global story isn't terribly different. In 2011 the Food and Agriculture Organization, a branch of the United Nations (an international peacekeeping and humanitarian organization), estimated that about one-third of all food produced for human consumption was wasted. This waste is particularly tragic because 795 million people on Earth don't have enough food to lead healthy, active lives.

Grocery stores are responsible for 10 percent of US food waste. Store managers want grocery store shelves to appear abundant and fully stocked at all times, so they buy more fruits, veggies, and other items than they can possibly sell. Their fear is that if consumers walk in and see nearly empty shelves, they'll assume that the store is subpar and shop elsewhere. So managers overbuy, restock shelves constantly, and remove any damaged or past-date items from the sales floor. Supermarket produce departments often pile up fruits and vegetables into pyramid shapes. Frequently, the food at the bottom of the pile becomes crushed or bruised. Although this food is safe to eat, store staff regularly remove and discard it. They want only the most appetizing produce in displays.

Wasted food has to go somewhere. Some consumers and communities put the waste to good use. They toss it into a container, where it decomposes and turns into compost. Compost can be fertile soil for farms and gardens. Because it's made of organic matter, it provides many nutrients for plants. Some restaurants and grocery stores donate unsold food to organizations that feed the hungry. But the vast majority of unsold food is carted off to landfills.

Unlike food tossed into a compost bin, food dumped into landfills doesn't benefit the ecosystem when it breaks down. It mixes in with toxic nonfood materials, such as cans of old paint, unused household cleaning fluids, and dead batteries that have not been recycled properly.

When it decomposes in landfills, food waste generates methane, a greenhouse gas that is twenty-five times more potent in trapping heat in our atmosphere than carbon dioxide. EPA studies have found that landfills produce 34 percent of all methane emissions in the United States. So that banana you brought for lunch, decided not to eat, and pitched into the cafeteria trash? It's contributing to global climate change.

GETTING AROUND AND STAYING PUT

Many discussions about minimalism focus on what we wear and eat, since both suck up loads of money and generate breathtaking amounts of waste. But transportation—getting from point A to point B—also creates waste and harms the planet.

You may be thinking, "Isn't minimalism about reduction? I can't cut back on the number of places I need to go. I can't magically shorten my daily routes." But you can choose less wasteful, greener ways to get around, and doing so reduces your personal impact in multiple ways.

Transportation pollution impacts our climate. Most people know that vehicle emissions are dirty and harmful. But even if you know that idling your hatchback with the heat on full blast is bad, let's review why. More than one-quarter of the greenhouse gases that US residents put into the atmosphere are belched out of our cars' tailpipes.

Transportation pollution doesn't just make Earth sick.

Bumper-to-bumper traffic crawls along in New York City. Gasoline-burning vehicles spew tons of pollutants into the air. One of them is carbon dioxide, a greenhouse gas that is a primary driver of climate change.

It makes the inhabitants sick too. Particles of soot and metals kicked into the air from exhaust pipes can become lodged deep into our lungs. Nitrogen oxides that float around in exhaust fumes can irritate the lungs and weaken the immune system—the network of cells and tissues that bodies use to fight infections and diseases. Pollutants such as hydrocarbons and carbon monoxide can harm the lungs and restrict the flow of oxygen throughout the body. Air pollution is also a leading cause of lung and bladder cancer.

These facts aren't meant to convince you to bike across town to visit your gran (unless you want to) or to walk 5 miles (8 km) to school every day (unless you can). They're meant to make you think twice about driving short distances when you could walk or about taking the bus when you could bike. Think reduction, not elimination.

Cheap home furnishings hurt too. Even if you've never spent your own money on a new dresser or desk lamp, you've likely helped pick out furniture and decorations for your bedroom. Like the fashion industry, the home furnishings industry is driven by an endless desire for cheap stuff. Furniture manufacturing involves dangerous chemicals, such as flame retardants applied to fabrics on couches and chairs. If factory workers aren't wearing protective gear—which they aren't in many poor nations—these chemicals can make them sick. (They can make consumers sick too. Flame retardants from consumer products have been linked to memory problems, cancer, and other health problems.) As with clothing manufacturers, many furniture manufacturers are in poorly constructed buildings. Fires and dangerous machinery are other hazards for workers. And curtains, comforters, and cushions that adorn your bedroom may come from big-box stores such as Walmart that buy inventory from overseas factories. In many of them, labor practices include eighteen-hour workdays and subpar wages.

The problem is more than working conditions. Furniture and home goods are the least recycled items in US households. When a chair or picture frame breaks, most Americans simply chuck it into the trash rather than repairing it. (It's possible to keep your space chic and fresh without adding a side order of guilt.)

STUFF = STRESS

Multiple studies show that living in cluttered environments, surrounded by mountains of stuff, makes people miserable. The Neuroscience Institute at Princeton University in New Jersey found that when people attempt to focus their minds while sitting in a room that's crammed with junk, they have a hard time completing tasks. Researchers at the University of California–Los Angeles studied thirty-two Los Angeles families and discovered that when mothers spent a lot of time buying, cleaning, reorganizing, and managing their belongings, they experienced an increase in stress hormones (body

Clutter does not just take up physical space. It can also clutter the mind, making it hard to focus and concentrate.

chemicals that make us feel anxious). That same study found that 75 percent of the families in the study had to park their cars in the driveway or on the street because their garages were too jam-packed with stuff.

When you consider all the negatives of the stuff we buy, show off, stash away, and then throw away, it's no wonder that minimalism is having a maximalist moment. Jumping on the minimalist bandwagon is about more than being a trend-savvy hipster. Living simply can help you feel better within your own life and have an impact on the future of our planet.

Enough whys—let's dig into the hows.

Vast amounts of donated clothing end up in Africa for resale. Here, shoppers buy secondhand clothing from the United States, Europe, and elsewhere at Gikomba Market in Nairobi, Kenya.

CHAPTER 3
GETTING STARTED

You might not need everything you currently own, but you do need some of your stuff. If you get rid of most of it in a single session—driven by a burning desire to be the best minimalist in the known universe—you will very likely regret it. You will probably have to rebuy some of the things you gave up. You might also miss some of the things you got rid of, which may make you resent and eventually abandon the idea of living simply. And you likely knew that chucking wearable clothes and usable furniture and electronics into the trash was not a green idea. But donating those items to thrift stores, secondhand stores, and charities doesn't automatically mean your stuff will go to a new owner. All over the world, but especially in the United States, people donate far more items than charity shops can possibly resell. Often these shops send unwanted furniture and broken electronics to landfills.

Clothing is a different story. Faced with an avalanche of old clothes, resale shops find ways to cope. They sell some of the excess clothing to companies that recycle it, turning it into materials such as insulation and carpet padding. The rest of the excess is bundled up and shipped overseas, mostly to Africa, for resale. Every year the United States exports more than 1 billion pounds (450 million kg) of used clothing. The majority of it ends up in used clothing markets in sub-Saharan Africa (African nations south of the Sahara). This may sound fine. But when African consumers have access to tons of cheap castoffs from the United States, African clothing manufacturers can't match the low prices. Many have gone out of business.

CONSIDER WHERE YOUR CASTOFFS WILL GO

Since Goodwill and Salvation Army can't sell all your old clothes, you must choose your donations carefully. Anything that's ripped, stained, or hopelessly misshapen is unlikely to be sellable, so set those items aside for repurposing or recycling. Items that are slightly off trend or that don't fit you anymore but are still in good condition are excellent candidates for donation. These rules also apply to electronics, home goods, artwork, and other things.

Consignment stores offer another great venue for finding your stuff a new home, with the added bonus of putting a little cash back in your pocket! Most consignment outlets focus on clothing, but some accept furniture, jewelry, and artwork too. If a consignment shop accepts your item for resale and succeeds in selling it, you'll get a percentage of the profits. The shops are picky about what they accept, though. You'll have the best luck selling relatively current clothing items that are free of flaws. Regardless of how you decide to jettison your stuff, ask yourself these two key questions first:

- Can these things be donated to a cause or person who can truly use them? The closer you are geographically to the group or individual who receives your used items, the more meaningful the donation becomes.
- Can I find a new home for these things without involving a retailer? Like grocery stores, secondhand stores often discard stuff that doesn't sell, which usually means sending it to landfills. So to increase the chances of your castoffs having a life beyond your initial ownership, give them directly to another human. Have a clothing swap at school or with friends, ask your online community if anyone could use the chair you're getting rid of, or chat with relatives about making use of your hand-me-downs.

Of course, it would be ideal to avoid overbuying in the first place. Whenever you shop, try to think about what you need versus what you want, and if you're going to buy something, think about what you could recycle, repurpose, or give away to make room for the new item. It can sometimes help defer or even nix a purchase you don't really need. Think critically about how to balance and prioritize your purchases so you end up with useful, lovable stuff that you want to keep—and not items that you'll soon end up throwing away. Minimizing responsibly can be challenging, but you can make it easier by thinking first about the impact of your actions. Think before you buy, and research before you donate.

HOW TO GET RID OF STUFF RESPONSIBLY

These are some fabulous ways to begin decluttering your life. Take things slowly, and go for the methods and venues that make sense for you and where you live. You might even want to ask a friend or a relative to help you declutter. Sometimes you need a second opinion to decide what to keep and what to let go of.

Online consignment. Do you have great clothes but no access to brick-and-mortar consignment stores? Try online outlets like thredup.com or Swap.com. You send your clothes to the company. If they are accepted, the company photographs and lists them for sale. Then you earn a percentage of the profits if they sell! But if your items are not accepted for sale, you might have to pay a fee for the company to ship them back to you or to donate them. Some sites require users to be eighteen or older, so check policies before listing your items. Ask a parent or guardian to help you if there is an age requirement.

Garage sale. If you're getting rid of clothing plus books, electronics, decorations, and other things, consider hosting a garage sale or stoop sale. If you live in an area with a lot of pedestrian traffic, put up a few signs on utility poles and neighborhood bulletin boards. You might want to advertise your sale on local neighborhood social media too. This can be a great way to sell your stuff and meet your neighbors! Don't have much to sell? Invite a few friends to sell their castoffs along with yours. Many neighborhoods have yearly block sales in the spring or summer. Check online to see if your neighborhood does. It can be an easy way to sell things without having to do the advertising yourself.

Clothing swap. Invite some friends over, crank up the music, and start digging through one another's castoffs! If your goal is to minimize your total number of clothes, limit yourself to taking one item for every three you offer to the swap pool. Don't worry if you and your friends have a variety of sizes, body shapes, and styles. If your size 8 bestie throws an oversized top into the mix, it might look amazing on your size 16 frame and vice versa. Your size 8 bestie may be looking for comfy, oversize items. Keep an open mind and experiment.

Online markets. The ever-growing world of online selling, including eBay, Poshmark, and Tradesy, are great ways to find

A clothing swap is a win-win-win. Participants get rid of clothing that no longer fits or suits them, they come home with new (to them) duds, and no clothes end up in the trash.

new homes for your goodies. You'll need to take your own photos, write your own descriptions, and manage your own listings. But you also get a much bigger percentage of the final purchase price than you would at a consignment shop. As with online consignment, check the site's policy to make sure you're old enough to sell. If you're not, ask for help from an adult.

Social media. Craigslist, Nextdoor, and Facebook Marketplace allow you to post information about items you're selling. Listings are free, but be cautious about meeting with strangers who express interest in your sale. Read the

MEET A MINIMALIST: LIFESTYLE BLOGGER SARAH VON BARGEN

Sarah Von Bargen blogs at yesandyes.org, a website that helps its readers live fuller, less stressful, more productive lives. The Minnesota-based writer is also a seasoned world traveler, thrifting wizard, and minimalist. Here are some of her thoughts about minimalism:

Why do you consider yourself a minimalist?
To be totally honest, I never really considered myself a minimalist till other people started calling me that. It just never occurred to me to keep things I don't use or don't like. It wasn't till a few years ago when friends would see my closet or shelves that the word *minimalist* came up. I was just making choices and living life in a way that made sense to me. And apparently it aligns with minimalism.

websites' policies about protecting your personal safety when you sell, and make sure that a parent or other trusted adult knows about your listing. If you're not in it for the money, consider Freecycle. On this online network, people list free stuff they want and free stuff they want to give away.

Community organizations. Most thrift stores are associated with a charity. Examples include Goodwill, Salvation Army, and Habitat for Humanity ReStore. They sell your used

What are some of the ways you try to live with less on a daily basis?

I bring travel mugs with me when I go to the coffee shop, I keep a refillable water bottle in my car, and I bring reusable grocery bags whenever I go shopping.

What's hardest about living this way?

I get the occasional snarky comment or defensive snap. A surprising number of people comment on it or seem to think I'm making my choices *at* them. I'm not fussed by anyone else's life choices—if you want to own seventy-five pairs of jeans, that's your business!

What's fun, rewarding, or awesome about living this way?

Life is a million times easier when you only own things you love that work well. You spend less time deciding what to wear, less time trying to find items, less time cleaning things, less time working in order to buy new things.

What advice would you give to someone who wants to create a smaller impact on Earth but isn't sure where to start?

Grab a box, set a timer, and go to one area of your house. Pick up one item at a time, and if you haven't used it in a year, if it has no sentimental value, put it in the box and then bring that box to Goodwill!

items, and part of the proceeds go to help people in need. But you can give your gently used clothes (or unworn new ones), towels, and bed linens to people in need directly. Call your city or county social services department (look online for the phone numbers) to find a nearby homeless shelter or women's or men's shelter. Ask what clothing or other items they need most, and take your items there. Local houses of worship also work directly with people in need or host sales.

Electronics contain toxic metals and chemicals, so they have to be recycled carefully. Here, workers dismantle old computers and other devices in Dobbspet, India.

Check out a church, temple, or mosque in your neighborhood to see if they will take used items.

Electronics recycling. Computers, smartphones, and televisions contain toxic metals, so it's important not to put your old ones in the trash. Many cities have electronics recycling drop-off centers, but some residents don't use them. They violate disposal service rules by throwing old electronics in the trash for curbside pickup. If old electronics end up in a landfill, the harmful metals will add to the toxic stew of garbage. If they end up in an incinerator, which will burn them, the toxins will enter the air in the form of harmful gases. Ideally, find someone who wants to use your old laptop or cell phone. But if it's no longer usable, find a reputable company to recycle it safely. Most urban areas have electronics recycling drop-off programs. Check your city government website, or call city hall to ask how to responsibly recycle your out-of-date technology. Or see if your neighborhood has a drop-off site for electronics.

Shopping secondhand is a smart minimalist choice. The clothes you buy get a second life, and the prices can't be beat.

CHAPTER 4

MINIMALIST BASICS FOR STUFF YOU BUY

The minimalist movement attracts a lot of smart people with strong opinions and specific ideas. Certain minimalists believe their own type of minimalism is the best and only way to live simply and responsibly. Don't let them scare you off. There is no one right way to be a minimalist.

If you want to limit your belongings but can't possibly pare your closet down to twenty items, that's fine. You may be determined to help Earth but can't afford expensive organic produce or clothing made with all-natural, organic fibers. There are other ways to be authentically minimalist. Whether you want to live more simply because stuff overwhelms you, because you want to protect the planet, or for another reason, embrace that urge. Easy, practical, and inexpensive ways to streamline your life and belongings are there to choose from. Ignore the ones you know won't work for you, adopt the ones that resonate with you, and customize any of them to suit your unique needs as a budding minimalist.

FASHIONABLE MINIMALISM MADE EASY

Fashion isn't always easy. But you can find easy ways to ensure that your clothing, shoe, and accessory shopping habits are minimalist-friendly and low waste.

Buy used. Depending on where you live, you may have access to dozens of fully stocked, beautifully organized thrift and consignment stores. You might only have a couple of lame charity shops or no secondhand shopping options within a 50-mile (80 km) radius. If you're living in a thrift-free zone, check out secondhand clothing websites. They can be a smart way to get rid of stuff and to purchase too.

Shopping at thrift stores can be a huge first step toward becoming a stylish minimalist. Used clothing is essentially recycled—it doesn't feed the fast-fashion machinery. By giving someone else's castoffs a second life, you're ensuring that the fuel, fabric, and human labor used to create them goes many times further.

TIPS FOR SECONDHAND SHOPPING

If you're a thrifting novice, scouring the racks at Savers or Goodwill can be incredibly overwhelming. Here are five guidelines to help you get started:

1. **Stack your discounts.** Before you head to the shop, check websites for coupons or deal days (50 percent off purple tags on Thursday, holiday-related discounts, and so on). If the store takes donations from the public, bring your giveaway pile. Some "swap shops" will give you a bag of deeply discounted clothing for every bag you donate. Other thrift stores will give you a discount coupon for donating. If the shop has a customer loyalty card, bring it! Some shops offer discounts after you've spent a certain amount.

2. **Dress smart.** Wear something that's easy to change into and out of, such as a dress and slip-on shoes, or wear a tee and slim pants as a bodysuit. Then if the store lacks dressing rooms or they're filled, you can try on some clothes in the aisles. If private fitting rooms are available, you'll be out quickly by avoiding lace-up boots and multiple layers.

3. Be strategic. Never thrift when you're exhausted, sad or angry, hungry, or in a hurry. Head out when you are relaxed and eager to shop so those jam-packed racks don't frustrate and frazzle you. Tackle the store section by section. Start with pants, and move on to skirts, dresses, sweaters, shirts, and outerwear. If you can't do it all, that's OK. Do one or two sections, and come back the next week.

4. Keep an open mind. Consider bringing a wish list of items to track down—but keep it pretty general. You're more likely to score looking for flannel shirts than large-print red plaid flannel shirts in 100 percent cotton. Even if you're seeking specific items, allow your eye to wander and bring a few adventure picks into the fitting room. You never know what kind of amazing items you may find.

5. Check for flaws. Always check every inch of a potential purchase for flaws. A three-dollar sweater isn't a bargain if it has a giant ink stain on the cuff that you don't notice until you get home. Durable goods such as blazers, outerwear, leather handbags, and jeans usually hold up to wear better than tees, dresses, and shirts. So if you're concerned about thrifted clothes falling apart, stick to these. If an item is damaged, but you still want it, bargain with the store staff. Prices at secondhand stores are seldom firm. Remember that you can replace missing buttons and sew loose seams.

Buying secondhand clothes also gives you access to a more varied pool of items. While everyone else is browsing the exact same stuff at Abercrombie or J. Crew, you're looking at clothes that may be several seasons, years, or even decades old! Mix some funky, eye-catching vintage pieces into your wardrobe for instant chic. Thrifting is an easy, affordable way to create a truly unique personal style.

Of course, you needn't buy everything you wear secondhand. Most people avoid thrifted undergarments. Others stay away from secondhand workout gear and shoes. If the idea of wearing someone else's stuff next to your skin makes your skin crawl, opt for outer layers such as jackets, vests, and coats. Or try accessories such as backpacks, purses, jewelry, watches, and neckties. Then eventually you might warm up to perfectly broken-in jeans, crushingly hip graphic tees, and darling retro dresses. Some of the items that come to secondhand stores—whether thrift, vintage, or consignment—are brand new. So you're getting a fabulous deal and helping out at the same time.

Repair damaged clothing. Stained T-shirts and jackets with blown-out elbows are *not* eligible for donation to charities. But that doesn't mean they have to go to the landfill, especially if they are longtime favorites. By mending or repairing damaged clothes, you extend their life. If you repair creatively, with fun contrasting fabrics or threads, you can even give them new life. Using your belongings for as long as possible is central to minimalist living. Here's a few repair pointers:

- You can dye clothes that are faded or lightly stained. Dye darker than the original garment color for best results. Rit and iDye are both reliable clothing dye brands.
- Bleach white clothes with stains. Ask for an adult's help since bleach is a strong, toxic chemical.
- Patch clothes with worn elbows and knees and torn pockets. Cut out a patch from a piece of cute contrasting fabric and sew it on. Or use an iron-on patch. Some people get creative with darning, knitting, and crocheting to repair frayed mittens, sweaters, caps, and other woven fabrics.
- Resew buttons onto coats, shirts, skirts, vests, and more. If you don't know how, check YouTube for simple tutorials.
- If you have sewing skills, you can fix loose threads, busted seams, or more complex repairs by hand or with a sewing machine. If you don't own one, a friend or relative might have one. Or makerspaces in your community probably will.

If you can't do it yourself, pros may be able to do it for you. Remember, though, that repairs and alterations sometimes can be expensive and challenging. So if you're thinking about altering (or buying) a gorgeous dress that's three sizes too big, think again. Altering it may be a complete redo for the tailor, and it will cost money and take time.

Just because an item of clothing tears, you don't have to toss it out. You might be able to stitch it up yourself or repurpose it.

Here are some repair pointers:

- A tailor can adjust the hem on pants that are too long or short. Same thing for skirts.
- A tailor can replace broken zippers on nearly all clothing. (Zippers aren't actually that hard to replace. Check YouTube for tutorials, and give it a whirl.)
- A skilled tailor might be able to reweave a sweater that's developed a hole. (This is a toughie, so call first before you haul all your moth-eaten knitwear down to the shop!)
- If your body has shifted in size or shape lately, a good tailor might be able to adjust your favorite clothes to fit your today body. It is *much* harder

to make a small garment bigger than it is to make a big garment smaller. But if your waist shrank a bit or your sleeves are feeling roomy, your clothes can be altered. No need to buy new.

- A shoe repair shop can resole shoes and boots with worn-out heels or soles. Ask the shop about adding small cleats to the toes and heels of boots and shoes to help them last longer.
- Many shoe repair shops also handle leather goods repairs, so a handbag with a busted clasp or strap, or a leather jacket with a torn seam might be fixable. If the leather has become stained or discolored, the shop might be able to dye it.
- Jewelers can replace watch batteries, reset gemstones, and perform all kinds of repairs to your earrings, necklaces, rings, and bracelets.

Upcycle. Upcycling involves repurposing damaged or old clothes (and other items) for new uses. A dress with a stain on the bust? Try wearing a pullover sweater with it to highlight the skirt. A sweatshirt that's collecting dust in your closet? Cut it down the front, hem the seams, adorn with sparkly buttons on one side of the cut, and you have a cute jacket. Cut up an old leather coat with a giant ink blotch, and transform it into a tote or backpack. Refashion a stained tee into a slogan or graphic tee with iron-ons or fabric markers. Turn tees and sweaters into cozy pillows. The possibilities are endless.

Check the blog *Upcycle That* (www.upcyclethat.com) for inspiration and ideas. Many of the tutorials focus on home decor and art projects, but some clothing projects are mixed in.

Research your brands. Minimalism often means living with less stuff, and usually that means buying less stuff. If using what you have just won't do and it's time for something new, buy from companies that use Earth-friendly fibers (such as organically grown cotton, linen, or bamboo) and that treat employees fairly.

Many companies, including Walmart and Forever 21, post sustainability statements on their websites. *Sustainability* is a twenty-first-century buzzword that encompasses everything from using alternative fuels to organic farming to protecting workers' rights. Companies' carefully written sustainability statements often make their brands sound like environmentally conscious saints. This is because eco-friendly is trendy, and companies know that aligning themselves with Earth-first ideals is good for their corporate images. So they craft language that says they'll "work harder to be more sustainable" or "prioritize safe factory conditions." Sometimes the statements don't actually tell you what the company is doing or not doing. In fact, Walmart and Forever 21 have been involved in multiple scandals over unsafe factory conditions, with former workers reporting that they sewed, ironed, or packed clothing six days a week for up to twelve hours a day while earning poverty wages.

Rather than relying on company claims, consult independent rating sites. Rank a Brand (rankabrand.org) is a Dutch website that conducts research into brand sustainability claims. It analyzes the results and creates a custom report and numerical ranking based on how eco-friendly the brands truly are. The site investigates climate change impact, environmental impact, and labor conditions before ranking a company. The smartphone app Good On You (goodonyou.eco) allows you to look at a brand's ethical ratings on the go.

Being an informed minimalist helps you find sustainable items. You'll be giving your money to worthy organizations and getting wardrobe items that will last a long time. While plenty of expensive clothes are made by workers who toil in unsafe conditions, many companies with low prices treat their laborers well and use organic fibers. Expensive doesn't mean good, and low cost isn't necessarily bad. Do your research so you can make informed buying decisions.

Use what you have. Probably you have some wardrobe items that were born in fast-fashion factories and crafted from synthetic materials. It's almost impossible to be a clothes-wearing human and not end up with some fast fashion in the mix. But if you will be buying less harmful clothes, consider what to do with those fast-fashion clothes you already own. Solution? Wear them—for as long as you possibly can, until they begin to fall apart. Then repair them.

Part of the problem with fast fashion is that it encourages people to give up on their clothes quickly. We buy them frequently to keep up with fashion crazes, and we get rid of them just as frequently. Then we buy even more clothes to replace the ones we've ditched. When we buy into this cycle, our consumer behavior tells clothing companies that we will keep snapping up low-price fashions season after season.

So treat all your clothes well, wash them carefully, and patch them. This will extend their lives, and you will be using fewer items. Then you will be helping to slow down the fast-fashion cycle.

HOW TO EAT LIKE A MINIMALIST

Minimalists are not constantly dieting. It's unnecessary to reduce the amount of food you eat to align yourself with minimalist ideas. You can eat like a minimalist and never feel hungry or deprived. The focus of minimalist eating is on buying what you need, using as much of it as possible, wasting very little, and composting what remains. Practices such as bringing your own tote bags to the grocery store, refilling and reusing glass or metal water bottles, buying in bulk to avoid excess packaging, and recycling any food packaging you can't avoid also help save resources and reduce garbage.

One of the keys to eating like a minimalist is planning your meals carefully, a tactic that can be challenging. The idea is to consider your food needs for the coming days or week, identify meals or recipes you want to make, and shop only for items that aren't in your fridge or pantry. If you don't do the shopping for your household, talk with a parent or guardian about how you can become more involved in meal planning and shopping. Your input and influence may shift how everyone in your family thinks about and consumes food.

Purchase food carefully. The first step toward becoming a minimalist eater is to reduce the amount of food you buy—and don't eat. So when you shop, consider what you really need and don't buy extra. This advice mostly applies to groceries, since we tend to buy more than we need and throw away plenty that's still edible. But it also applies to eating out. Restaurants purchase massive amounts of food. That's because they must have everything on the menu available to prepare, even if customers don't order it. Many restaurants serve huge portions that people don't finish. Leftovers could be composted, but more often, they're thrown away. So when you order at a restaurant, consider how much you actually want and need to eat. If you order too much, can't eat the giant portions, and know the food will keep well for a day or two, take your leftovers home in a doggie bag.

Use leftovers. Minimalists typically do their best to eat the overflow from previous meals. Whether you have stew from a batch your parents cooked or half a burger stashed in the fridge from a couple of days ago, consider reheating it. Or combine it in creative ways with other ingredients to make a different meal before cooking something completely new.

The internet offers a nearly infinite supply of recipes designed to use leftovers. Pinterest is phenomenal for cooking ideas. Pop "leftover recipes" into its search bar, and view the mouthwatering results. Or use your favorite search engine to look for some recipe roundups. Greatist.com has a marvelous

Fighting food waste can be as simple as using up all the leftovers in your fridge.

post titled "65 Amazing Meals You Can Make from Leftovers Today." It has suggestions for cooking with everything from leftover pasta and bread to surplus meat and fruit. In 2016 the FYI Network launched the TV series *Scraps*, on which chef Joel Gamoran creates menus from leftovers and frequently tossed food items. Episodes online offer waste-free inspirations.

If you have a pet, some leftover ingredients make great treats. Many veggies and meats are safe for dogs, cats, and even birds. Do some research to learn what'll work best for your furred or feathered friend. Certain foods, including chocolate, coffee, avocados, coconuts, and citrus fruits, can harm and even kill pets. Check out the article "People Foods to Avoid Feeding Your Pets" on the American Society for the Prevention of Cruelty to Animals website before you feed Fido leftovers.

Buy local, buy organic. Reducing your eco-impact as a minimalist also means thinking carefully about what you buy and where it comes from. Focus on purchasing locally grown food. Then you are supporting your community growers. The food doesn't travel over hundreds or thousands of miles by train or truck, burning fossil fuels. Organically farmed and grown food can be a good option too. Organic farming is far less harmful to the soil, water, and environment than conventional farming. When you purchase organically grown foods, you support the farmers who choose this Earth-friendly method. Organic farms are usually small operations, without the efficiencies of large industrial farms. Organic farmers do more work by hand. They take better care of farm animals, usually by making sure they have space to move and lots of natural light. By rejecting pesticides and herbicides, they also take better care of the soil and water than conventional farmers do.

All this adds up to higher costs for the organic farmer, so you can expect to pay more for organic food. But as organic food becomes more popular, prices are dropping. Even many chain stores, including Target and Aldi, offer organic produce at affordable prices. Often farmers markets sell locally grown and organic foods at reasonable prices as well.

Many restaurants specialize in organic cuisine, and others highlight menu items that include locally produced, organic ingredients. Whenever you order organic, you are eating like a minimalist. But even if you buy all organic food, you need to watch how much you purchase. No free passes on wasting edibles!

Instead of throwing away food scraps, consider adding them to a compost pile. After the food decays, you'll have nutrient-rich soil for your garden.

Compost. Composting food waste involves letting it decay in a bin or pile, similar to the decay that occurs in nature. Composters place food scraps in a heap, along with other organic matter, such as paper, frozen ice sticks, and coffee filters (all of which are made from wood pulp, a natural substance). Composters add soil and water to the mix, and tiny microorganisms in the soil break down the organic matter. The result is humus. It contains substances such as nitrogen, phosphorus, and potassium, which are fuel for plants. Humus is an excellent fertilizer to enrich soil in gardens and croplands.

If you have a yard or garden, you can create a compost heap right on the ground. You can also buy a premade composting bin from a hardware store. If the compost pile is turned over and watered regularly, you might have finished compost in as little as two to three weeks. (Untended compost can take months to transform into humus, and plant materials may take even longer to decompose in the wild.)

Because the decaying food in a compost pile can be smelly and attract bugs, most people keep compost piles outside (although odor-free indoor bins are available). If you don't have a yard, you might find a citywide composting program with free weekly pickup of compostable materials from household bins. The compost goes to local farms or gardens. Composting is a fantastic way to reduce the amount of food waste in landfills. It is also an environmentally friendly practice, since the food in a compost bin decomposes safely and helps new plants grow. Check online to see if your community has a composting program.

Many public spaces compost food as well. Public schools, colleges, and universities are composting food waste from cafeterias. Some airports, restaurants, and parks have composting bins too. Look for composting bins wherever you go.

Recycle food containers. Probably, you've been recycling at home and at school. But if you aren't, it's time to start. Recycling cans, bottles, boxes, bags, and other food containers keeps them out of the landfill and ensures they'll be used again or reused in other ways. Recycle as much as you can as often as you can.

MAKING YOUR SPACE MORE MINIMAL

The only personal space for many teens is their bedroom—
and some may share it with a sibling or two. There, you can
express yourself—by decorating the walls with posters of your
favorite bands and covering your desk with meaningful gifts
from friends. You might not want to put constraints on how that
space can look. But here are several ways to build a minimalist
space for yourself and have room for full self-expression. If you
share a bedroom, you can collaborate with your siblings on
a shared minimalist space. If they don't want to, you can still
make minimalist choices for your part of the room.

Decorate with sustainable items. Bedroom basics often
mean a bed, a desk, a chair, and maybe a bookcase. Assuming
you have some or all of those in your room, you don't have to
ditch them for eco-friendlier versions. As with clothes, using
your furniture for as long as you possibly can keeps it out of
the landfill and keeps demand for new furniture lower. But if
you ever have to replace your furniture or add a piece you've
always needed or are decorating (or redecorating) your space,
consider sustainable options.

Figuring out sustainability for furniture and room
decorations isn't always easy. But when buying wooden
furniture, look for products approved by the Forest
Stewardship Council (FSC). In its approved forests, managers
don't use pesticides. They don't cut down vast stands of
trees, leaving the soil bare and more likely to wash away in
storms. They respect and protect the animals and plants that
rely on the forest ecosystem.

Other sustainable furniture is made from reclaimed, recycled, or upcycled materials, such as old barn wood or the flooring from an old building. Usually furniture companies will highlight eco-friendly practices in their catalogs and other marketing materials. If you're not sure, ask a salesperson or email the company a question.

Upcycle. Even better than buying upcycled furniture and decor is doing the upcycling yourself. You can turn beloved old T-shirts, flannel shirts, or sweaters into pillows and quilts. Old wood pallets can become platform beds, upside-down wire wastebaskets can become nightstands or plant stands, and metal pails can become lampshades. Pinterest is a gold mine for ideas. Thrift stores, garage sales, military surplus shops, and even curbside on garbage pickup day will offer most of the raw materials you need. You can even dig through your own basement for items that are screaming to be reborn into fun and funky pieces of furniture for your room.

Secondhand furniture and decor. If you're slightly less crafty but still love giving items a new life, see what you can nab secondhand. Thrift stores and garage sales are great resources. So are antique stores, flea markets, estate sales, Nextdoor, Craigslist, eBay, and Facebook Marketplace. You can buy all kinds of used items, from desk chairs to drapery. Prices will be similar to what you'd pay at big-box discount stores, but the items you get will be preloved. By giving them a new home, you save them from the landfill and the incinerator.

EASY UPCYCLING PROJECTS FOR YOUR HOUSE

Wine Cork to Succulent Magnet

Materials
peel-and-stick magnets
wine corks
glue
scissors
dirt
small succulent plants
tweezers (optional)

1. Secure a magnet to the side of each cork. Even with peel-and-stick magnets, add some glue for a secure attachment.

2. Carefully use the scissors to make a hole in each cork where the corkscrew had been inserted. Create a space about 0.25 inches (0.6 cm) deep and about the same width.

3. Fill the holes with dirt.

4. Using tweezers, if necessary, gently tuck a succulent plant into each hole.

5. Attach the magnets to the refrigerator or another metal surface.

Old Jeans to Heart-Shaped Bookmarks

Materials
a ruler or measuring tape

a fabric pencil or piece of white chalk

an old pair of jeans

scissors

a small piece of wax paper or other nonstick paper

a 1-inch (2.5 cm) brush

fabric glue or Mod Podge craft glue (matte finish)

3 strands of embroidery thread or 1 strand of lightweight yarn

a needlepoint needle (strong enough to work through two pieces
of denim and with an eye that is wide enough for the thread or
yarn of your choice)

1. With a ruler or measuring tape and a fabric pencil or piece of chalk, measure out and mark two 3 inch x 3 inch (7.6 cm x 7.6 cm) squares on the wrong side of your fabric.

2. Cut out the squares. Then fold them in half separately on the diagonal (bottom left corner toward top right corner).

3. One at a time, carefully cut the diagonal cloth into a heart shape. Start by holding the diagonal with the fold between the thumb and fingers of one hand. Then take the scissors in the other hand and cut the curved shape of the top of a heart, cutting from the top of the fold around and down toward the center of the open side of the diagonal.

4. Place the nonstick paper and fabric on a flat working surface. Using the brush, coat the fabric hearts with glue on both sides. This will keep the fabric from fraying at the edges. Allow the fabric to dry for at least 60 minutes.

5. When the hearts are completely dry, thread your needle. Sew the two hearts together, right sides facing out, stitching along the outside straight edges of the fabric. Leave the curved top open.

6. When you are done stitching, slide the needle and thread through three stitches on the back of the heart and clip the thread. Place the open, curved top of the heart over the corner of a page. You've got a bookmark!

MINIMALIST DESIGN

If you'd like to create a serene, uncluttered space for yourself, try minimalist design guidelines. Less stuff in your space can reduce your stress levels—and the results will be visually striking.

Edit what you have. Focus on getting rid of excess and making more use of the things you love, need, and enjoy. Pare down to items that you truly need and minimize cluttered shelves, floor space, and other surfaces. But don't chuck anything that is meaningful, practical, or important to you. It's better to edit slowly over a long period, tackling the purge in waves. You might also consider a one-in, one-out policy. If you buy a fantastic new desk lamp for your space, donate or sell your current desk lamp so that you keep only one of each type of furniture.

Decide what will remain visible. Although the end goal is to rid your space of excess, you don't have to get rid of everything. You might decide to keep your beloved knickknacks but store them out of sight. A minimalist space is clean and spare, with few items out in the open. You can stash and organize your stuff in closets, storage boxes under beds, or lidded containers. Choose which artwork will adorn the walls, which essential items will sit on your desk, and which pillows and toys will get places of honor on your bed. Keep what you want, and hold onto what you love. Leave visible only things that need to be accessed easily or that create the visual vibe you want. Periodically rotate items to change the feel while still keeping a spare look.

To design like a minimalist, mix a few favorite colors with more neutral tones.

Choose a color scheme. In magazine and online articles about minimalism, you'll notice that many minimalist bedrooms feature neutral colors. White, black, brown, and gray are easy on the eyes and can create a beautiful backdrop for a streamlined room. But you can have a pink, turquoise, or chartreuse minimalist bedroom if you want. The key is to keep your color scheme simple. Limit the colors of the walls, window frames, and big pieces of furniture to three if possible. If you love pink, for example, pick one or two tones of pink for the walls and your bedspread. Keep everything else in the room, such as chairs and bookcases, white. If you like a bright color such as turquoise, use it as an accent. Paint one wall turquoise, and choose a bedspread, piece of artwork, or comfy chair for the second turquoise element in the room. Then use a light turquoise or pale contrasting color such as lavender for the other walls and your rug. If you need help, take some photos of your space and bring them to your local paint store. The salesclerks there know all about bedroom color schemes. They will discuss color options. Some paint company websites even allow you to upload images of your room and play with color options.

Create visual harmony. Once you have eliminated clutter, look around your space. What can you do to make it feel even more cohesive, peaceful, and welcoming? If you have bookshelves, consider organizing your books by spine color or by size. Cluster framed photos together so they look more like a single item and less like individual images strewn around the space. Consider moving your dresser inside your closet, where it will still be accessible but hidden from view. Experiment by moving furniture around within the space to see where each piece feels most natural. For example, one major design basic is to avoid placing all your furniture along the walls. This creates an empty space in the middle of the room. Instead, try placing your desk at an angle in a corner or creating a reading nook using a squishy armchair and side table angled together.

You'll have a much easier time creating a visually minimal bedroom if your big furniture pieces are fairly sleek and simple themselves. But ornate brass bed frames and bold printed curtains can work—if they are the only shiny, busy pieces in the space. If you already have some decidedly non-minimalist furniture in your room, don't feel obliged to drain your piggy bank to buy new stuff. Declutter, rearrange, and make the space as open and clean as you can. If you can't create the magazine-worthy minimalist bedroom of your dreams, you can still get close in a way that celebrates your dedication to simplification.

To dry clothes the old-fashioned way, hang them in the yard. The sun and wind will do the job, and you won't use any fuel running a gas or electric dryer.

CHAPTER 5

MINIMALIST BASICS FOR STUFF YOU USE

Many people think of minimalism as a stuff-centric concept that's only about owning fewer tangible things. Most minimalist living has that as a goal. But minimalism is not just about owning less. It's also about using less.

POWERING DOWN

You can control your electricity and power usage in ways that don't involve limiting Snapchat time to five minutes a day.

Here are some great ways to start:

Turn off the lights. You need light to read and to navigate around your space. But if you are leaving a room and no one else is there, turn off the lights. If a room is already flooded with natural light, leave the lamps off. According to the Energy Resource Center, a Colorado energy-conservation organization, Americans waste 61 to 86 percent of the energy that flows through our shared power lines. For example, we leave electric appliances and lights on even when we're not actively using them. As a minimalist, you can help improve that statistic. All it takes is the flick of a switch.

Turn off your computer. It's so convenient to have your computer constantly on or in sleep mode. All you have to do is wake it up with a jiggle of the mouse. But idle computers suck up energy, and that energy adds up. Studies show that leaving computers on overnight wastes billions of dollars in energy costs. Many of the plants that generate electricity burn coal and natural gas kick millions of tons of carbon dioxide into the atmosphere. So turn that computer off. It'll take less than three minutes to turn it back on again in the morning.

Do things the old-fashioned way. Line-dry clothes instead of tossing them into the electric dryer. Wash dishes by hand instead of running them through the electric dishwasher. Mash potatoes using your own strength (and a handheld mashing tool) instead of the electric mixer. In the winter, put on a sweater, a cap, and some warm slippers instead of cranking up the heat. In the summer, pull the shades and use fans instead of the air conditioner. When you do run it on a hot day, keep it above 78°F (26°C). Anything lower will eat vast amounts of energy (and result in a big electricity bill). For small yards, mow with a push mower instead of a gas mower. In the winter, shovel by hand instead of using a snowblower. It's great exercise! Patience and elbow grease are two underrated ways to conserve power!

CONSERVING WATER

Did you know that 95 percent of the water Americans use goes down the drain? Or that Americans use 127 percent more water than in the 1950s? Many Americans tend to think of water as an endless, easy-access resource. The World Health Organization (part of the United Nations) says that climate change, population growth, and urbanization all challenge water supply systems worldwide. Much of the drinkable water on Earth comes from underground pools called aquifers. As cities grow, as droughts become more common, and as croplands expand, we are draining and polluting them. One of the most vital aquifers in the United States is the Ogallala Aquifer. It lies under eight midwestern states and provides water mainly for farms but also for homes and businesses. We've already used up 30 percent of the water in the aquifer, and another 39 percent will be gone by the mid-twenty-first century. Other aquifers are running dry too, so we need to conserve water. Here are three home water-saving practices:

Turn off the tap. When we're brushing teeth or doing the dishes, we sometimes forget that we have the tap on full blast and that gallons of unused water are gushing down the drain. The EPA estimates that turning off the tap while brushing your teeth can save 8 gallons (30 L) of water a day. Shutting it off while shaving can save 10 gallons (38 L) of water per shave. If you brush your teeth twice a day and shave five times a week, you could save nearly 5,700 gallons (21,575 L) a year. Multiply that by millions of people, and that's millions of gallons of water each year.

Curb endless showers. Same concept but it can be a little harder to apply—especially if twenty minutes under a hot tap is your favorite way to wake up on school day mornings. Heating water burns fossil fuels (your home water heater probably burns natural gas), and long showers waste water. A standard showerhead spits out 2.5 gallons (9.4 L) of water every minute, so imagine five one-half gallon milk jugs full of water going to waste every sixty seconds. To save water, give yourself a few minutes to enjoy the shower, but limit that time. Showers should be for washing hair and body parts. Limit the amount of time (and water) you use to tackle those tasks. If you love baths, consider pouring a bucketful of the dirty bathwater on your garden, lawn, houseplants, or trees when you're done. Used sink and tub water—called gray water since it's slightly dirty—is safe for plants.

MINIMALIST BASICS FOR STUFF YOU USE

Rainwater runs from a gutter spout into a backyard rain barrel. Most rain barrels have a faucet at the bottom. By attaching a hose to the faucet, residents can direct the rainwater from the barrel to lawns and gardens.

Install a rain barrel. Possibly the greediest consumers of water are lawns and gardens. The EPA says that watering an average-sized lawn for twenty minutes every day for a week is the equivalent of running the shower constantly for four straight days or taking more than eight hundred showers. Instead of using tap water to keep your flowers and grass looking healthy, consider installing a rain barrel. Set beneath gutters, rain barrels capture rainwater running off roofs. The amount you can collect depends on how many barrels you have and the size of your roof. Suppose you've set up a rain barrel outside a 12 foot x 10 foot (3.65 m x 3 m) sunporch and a passing rainstorm drops 1 inch (2.5 cm) of rain. That's 75 gallons (284 L) of water for watering plants or washing cars. (Captured rainwater is not for drinking or for vegetable gardens, however, since it sometimes picks up contaminants from roofs and other human-made structures.) Many hardware stores sell rain barrel kits that are easy to assemble. Apartment dwellers can install smaller barrels on patios and balconies. Talk to a parent or guardian about whether a rain barrel would work where you live.

MINIMIZING MEDIA CONSUMPTION

Watching less TV, streaming fewer videos, and spending less time scrolling through the apps on your phone are all ways to save energy. Concentrating your device use into longer sessions instead of constantly turning your phone on and off to check it throughout the day can conserve battery power. That means less charging and less energy consumed. Don't be afraid to set boundaries for yourself, but make sure you can live with them so you give up and decide that minimalism doesn't work for you. When you aren't using your device or desktop, turn it off. In sleep mode, a device is still using energy. By turning it off, you save energy, and it takes just a couple of minutes to get started the next time.

Media encompasses a whole world of readables and watchables. Here are other ways to become a media-savvy minimalist:

Recycle old magazines. Magazines and catalogs are energy-intensive to produce. Writing and editing them on computers sucks up electricity. They're printed on tons of paper, using machines that run on fossil fuels. The delivery trucks that bring them to your neighborhood also run on fossil fuels. The good news is that they're recyclable. You can put them out for pickup with your aluminum cans and paper bags. Or you can give them a new life by gifting them to doctor's offices, hair salons, or community reading programs. Or consider upcycling them into collages, decoupage projects, or multimedia artworks. Think about saying no thank you from the get-go. Call or email companies to tell them that you do not want to receive their catalogs. Have them take your name off their mailing lists.

Sell or share books when you're through reading them. Libraries are fantastic resources for finding reading materials. But we still sometimes buy books and receive them as gifts. When books start to pile up, you can sell them to a used bookstore or at a garage sale. Or you can donate them to public libraries or thrift stores, or circulate them through the Little Free Library program (littlefreelibrary.org). This book exchange program encourages residents to swap and share

This Little Free Library station in San Francisco, California, is filled with books. Neighbors load up the box with books they no longer want, and other neighbors pick them up for free.

old books at small book stations. Look for a book station in your neighborhood, or think about building one if there isn't one near your home.

Be an informed media consumer. Living a minimalist life is hard when you're bombarded by a steady stream of messages about getting, buying, and having more stuff. Magazines, television and radio commercials, catalogs, and websites constantly urge consumers to shop. Mindfully minimizing your exposure to spend-centric media can help you reduce the amount of stuff you feel you have to buy. Being an informed consumer when you shop—making choices that are Earth-friendly and that reflect what you really need rather than making impulse purchases—will help you keep the things you own from owning you.

MINIMIZE PLASTIC

Everything you buy might be secondhand, recyclable, or organic, but you're not doing Earth any favors if those purchases are wrapped in plastic. Stores hand us plastic shopping bags, beverages come in plastic bottles, and many foods and consumer goods come in plastic packages. Plastic that hasn't been recycled or disposed of properly litters our oceans, rivers, and roadways. Some of the substances found in plastic have been linked to cancer and other illnesses. So the less plastic you use, the better. Here are some ways to reduce plastic waste:

Bring your own bottle. Instead of purchasing water in plastic bottles, fill a metal water bottle from your tap at home. Carry it with you, and refill it when it's empty.

Bring your own bag. Keep a cloth tote bag in your backpack or handbag. Use it for your purchases instead of accepting the plastic bag handed out at the cash register.

Wrap food without plastic. Instead of disposable plastic lunch bags, pack food in reusable glass or metal containers. Reusable wax-coated cloths are eco-friendly alternatives to plastic food wrap.

BOOMERANG BAGS

In 2013 Tania Potts and Jordyn de Boer, two environmentally minded women from the Gold Coast, Australia, joined forces to reduce plastic bag use in their hometown. They created reusable cloth bags out of recycled materials and gave them to family and friends. They named their organization Boomerang Bags, and within a few years, their model for crafting reusable bags had spread across the globe. Participating in the program is fun, free, and a great way to combat the harmful overuse of plastic bags. Here's how you can join the movement:

1. Visit boomerangbags.org to find a group, or start your own.

2. Collect materials from your home. Look for worn-out items made from durable fabric that you can cut up and upcycle. Or stock up on items like pillowcases, sheets, and tablecloths from thrift stores.

3. Meet with your group for a bag-making session. Boomerang Bags offers templates for bags, or you can create your own design.

4. Give away the bags you've made. Stash a few in your car for your own shopping trips, but give others to family, friends, teachers—and even strangers! On their website, the Boomerang cofounders say, "However you choose to distribute your bags, the most important thing is to ensure that they're distributed with a message about waste, about sustainability, about community. Make the connection and empower and inspire people to be part of the solution!"

If you're visiting Denver, Colorado, and need to get across town, the B-cycle program offers an Earth-friendly option. For a fee, you can unlock one of these bikes, pedal to your destination, and lock up the bike at another B-cycle station. Stations are located all over the city, at museums, restaurants, parks, and sports venues. Many cities across the country have similar bike-rental programs.

TRAVELING LIKE A MINIMALIST

Gasoline-powered vehicles are one of the main culprits in climate change. You can get where you need to without them or by using them selectively in low-impact ways.

Bike or walk. If you're a minimalist, these are the top two options. Neither burns fuel, requires electricity, nor has any measurable negative impact on Earth. Depending on where you live, biking to a friend's house might be a herculean 25-mile (40 km) endeavor and walking to the store might mean weaving through unsafe neighborhoods. You may not feel safe walking or biking late at night either. So use good judgment. Walk or bike where and when it's safe and smart to do so.

If you don't own a bike, flea markets, garage sales, and online swap sites have affordable used bikes. Many cities have bike rental programs with sturdy bicycles for an hourly fee or seasonal pass that you return to a shared bike rack. Rental programs are ideal for a quick jaunt across town.

Take public transit. After walking or biking, your next best option is to ride in a vehicle that's also carrying many other people—like a train or bus. When people share rides, they reduce the amount of fuel used, the number of vehicles on the road, and the amount of air pollution created. Many public buses run on natural gas or electricity, which are less

Electric buses help the environment in two ways. First, a busload of people traveling to one destination uses much less fuel than many people driving to that destination in their own individual cars. Second, electric vehicles don't spew carbon dioxide and other pollutants into the atmosphere. This electric bus is in Dorchester in the United Kingdom.

MINIMALIST BASICS FOR STUFF YOU USE

polluting than gasoline. Subways produce about 76 percent fewer greenhouse gas emissions per passenger mile than the average car. If you have access to public transportation, take it whenever you can! Public transportation is less expensive. You don't have to pay for gas or parking.

Carpool. If cars are the only way, see if you can ride with a friend or offer to drive friends in your car. Apps like GoKid and Kid Carpool can help you and your parents find others in your school who are open to sharing rides. The concept is the same as with public transit: the more people moved by a single vehicle, the better.

Invest in a fuel-efficient car. If you're in the market for a new car, investigate affordable car models that get good gas mileage (the number of miles traveled per gallon of gas). The less gas a car uses, the better it is for the environment. Big pickup trucks and SUVs are usually less fuel efficient than smaller cars, and cars with a manual transmission (stick shift) burn less fuel than automatics—although they can be tricky to learn to drive.

Hybrid (gas-burning combined with electric) cars emit fewer pollutants than all-gasoline cars, and all-electric options don't emit pollutants at all. These cars are too expensive for most families, but prices are falling as they become more popular and widely available.

Don't let the car idle. If you have to drive by yourself or be driven by a parent, be aware of how long the car is left running while standing still. You may have heard that restarting your engine burns more fuel than idling, but the

Environmental Defense Fund (EDF), a US environmental protection organization, disagrees. According to its research, idling for ten seconds wastes more gas than restarting the engine. The organization also says that an idling car releases 1 pound (0.5 kg) of carbon dioxide into the air every ten minutes. That's reason enough to stop idling!

As you let the minimalist mind-set sink in and get used to living with less, you'll start finding your own creative ways to reduce and streamline your everyday activities.

MINIMALISM FOR THE MAXIMALIST

You've collected and cultivated the perfect wardrobe for years, and the idea of donating any of it makes your head pound. Here are ways to fold minimalism into your fashion-forward lifestyle:

Wear each item you own and often. Most of us wear only a fraction of the clothing we own. That makes the other items theoretically unnecessary. If you haven't worn a certain sweater in six months, maybe you can part with it. But any clothing that is both loved and used is not excess. A large and varied wardrobe is only wasteful if the majority of things in it go unworn. So maximalists should feel free to keep their clothing collections intact but try to wear everything they own as often as possible. Wear everything—no exceptions, no excuses.

Set up a rotation system. At the beginning of each season, line up your pants, skirts, dresses, and shirts in your closet in an order that makes sense to you. On day 1, wear the first thing in line. At the end of the day, put it at the back of the line. On day 2, wear the next thing and so on. After taking a stab at wearing the entirety of your wardrobe, see what you've worn—and what you found impossible to wear. You may not actually need everything in your closet. Donate what you didn't wear.

Try a capsule wardrobe challenge. A capsule wardrobe is a small group of clothes you select from your closet and wear exclusively for a set time. This low-risk personal challenge is a fun way to see how creative you can get with a limited number of pieces. It also reinforces the idea that most of us can live incredibly fashionable lives using just a handful of key items.

Mend and repurpose. Minimalists select the things they buy with great care and then take great care of the things they own. Apply this principle to your closet by keeping your clothes, shoes, and accessories in fantastic shape. If something becomes ripped or stained, don't automatically toss it. Get creative about mending, upcycling, and giving damaged items a second chance.

Shop secondhand. Thrift stores are a fantastic place to get great clothes at affordable prices. Most items are less than five years old so the colors and cuts are still chic. Even if you can't bear the thought of a Zara-free existence, you can still shop secondhand. You'll find almost all fast-fashion brands at thrift stores or on websites such as eBay and thredup. In some thrift shops, you'll even find unused items. Retail stores often donate excess stock that they haven't been able to sell. And some shoppers buy too much and donate what they haven't worn.

MINIMALIST CHALLENGE: THE CAPSULE WARDROBE

The capsule wardrobe challenges you to wear stuff that typically goes unworn and reminds you that you don't actually need fifteen pairs of jeans to be stylish. Here are some parameters:

- Select thirty-five items from your closet, including school clothes, shoes, and outerwear. (Workout clothes, accessories, handbags, swimsuits, and undergarments aren't part of this exercise.) If possible, store all your other clothes out of sight.
- Consider creating a theme for your capsule to give it focus. Perhaps you'd like to explore your inner rocker or romantic. Create a capsule wardrobe that aligns visually with those aesthetics.
- Balance basics with fun pieces. If you pick thirty-five items that all have wild prints, you might end up frustrated.
- When in doubt, pick more tops than bottoms, since bottoms are more basic and versatile. You can wear the same skirt or pair of pants several times a week, mixing and matching with different tops and accessories, without anyone noticing.
- Create a color scheme, so that most items match the others in the selection.
- Commit to wearing only combinations of these thirty-five items for a month.

When the month is up, write a paragraph about your experience. What was harder than you'd expected? What was easier? How often did you wish you had access to your entire wardrobe? Would you do it again?

If you answered yes to the last question, pick another thirty-five items and begin again anytime. Invite a friend to do it with you!

MINIMALISM FOR COLLECTORS AND SENTIMENTALISTS

The things we own can be very meaningful. Many physical objects carry intense emotional payloads that can be hard to ignore and harder to give up. This is especially true for items that come from people we loved deeply but who are no longer in our lives or who have died. It's also true for nostalgia lovers and collectors. A paring down of belongings may just feel too painful or invasive. Remember that you should never get rid of things that you adore, that evoke important memories, or that you can't imagine living without. But if you feel as if you might be ready to let go a little, here are some ways to start:

Try Marie Kondo's "spark joy" technique. In *The Life-Changing Magic of Tidying Up*, best-selling author Marie Kondo outlines a simple technique for deciding whether to keep an item or to let it go. Pick it up, hold it in your hands, and then ask yourself, "Does this item spark joy?" That is, do you feel lit up inside when you are in physical contact with this object? If joy is sparked, the item stays. If not, you thank it for its service to you and put it in a pile for donations. This is a gut-level way to check in and make sure that your belongings actually belong in your space. Kondo recommends applying this test to everything you own as a way of identifying the keepers and weeding out the impostors. Yes, it takes a long time, but it's worth it. Do it slowly over time, and you'll be amazed by the progress you make!

Document items before getting rid of them. Still leery of putting anything in the donate pile? Even things that don't "spark joy"? Consider documenting their existence before letting them go. Photographing knickknacks, souvenirs, artwork and other framed items, clothes, and shoes that you have enjoyed but are thinking about letting go of can help you preserve the associated memories. Writing a little blurb about their history to accompany the images takes this preservation a step further. Keep the words and photos in an electronic scrapbook on your computer. Or make a paper scrapbook to commemorate the things you've loved, used, and passed along to a new owner.

Marie Kondo, author of *The Life-Changing Magic of Tidying Up*, helps others declutter their homes. Here she sorts through a client's possessions at a home in Tokyo, Japan.

Regular yoga and meditation practices are great ways to clear the mind and reduce stress.

CHAPTER 6
LIVING SIMPLY AS A LIFE PHILOSOPHY

While it's true that minimalism is about buying, having, eating, and creating less stuff, it's also about crafting a life that feels authentic and worthwhile. Releasing things that clutter your space is important. It can be equally rewarding to release activities and people who clutter your heart and mind. Embracing minimalism can make you feel less stressed, more centered, and more grounded in your life. As you begin to shift toward living with less, you can start to apply that philosophy to other parts of your life.

IDENTIFY YOUR STRESSORS

Life will always present stressors that you can't control or avoid: school, obnoxious people, health concerns, political and societal conditions you don't agree with, or a crush that ignores you. But you can handle other challenges. If your parents are gung ho for you to keep playing hockey but you would rather try soccer, have an honest discussion about your preferences. If you think taking four AP classes might make your head explode, be open about that. If your friends do things or take risks that make you uncomfortable or simply don't interest you, take charge and suggest other group activities.

Start by making a list of the things that worry or overwhelm you. Divide them into the situations you can and can't change. Manage your list by tackling the issues that you can impact, one small or main thing at a time. Ask for help if you need or want it. A friend or a trusted adult can be a good support and help you as you make changes. Over time, you'll find yourself feeling more relaxed and less like the world is closing in on you.

LET GO OF FRIENDSHIPS THAT WEIGH YOU DOWN

Probably, you have a friend or two who has stuck around for ages—maybe too long. Frenemies, childhood friends with whom you no longer have anything in common, drama-magnet friends who love making mayhem—anyone who drains your energy can be a candidate for gentle removal from your life.

MEET A MINIMALIST: ANTHONY UNGARO

Anthony Ungaro is the creator of *Break the Twitch*, a blog and YouTube channel about mindful living through minimalism, habits, and creativity. Here are his thoughts about minimalism:

Why do you consider yourself a minimalist?

I consider myself a minimalist because I'm constantly adjusting and editing my life to reflect my values and priorities. I don't believe that there is any particular point or number of items a person needs to have to be a real minimalist, but I do believe it's more of a filter to decide what comes in and out of our lives. We get to choose exactly what that means, but as it stands, I believe the philosophy of active decision-making is an effective way to be a minimalist, in addition to not owning so much stuff that it gets in the way of the life you actually want to be living.

What are some of the ways you try to live with less on a daily basis?

It's funny for me to see the words *live with less*, because every decision [my wife and I have] made around minimalism has ended up giving us a life with more. We focus on not bringing new unnecessary things into our home, which can be difficult at times. Making sure that if new things come in, we reassess what we already have to make sure it all still fits into the picture of what we want. We actively try to spend less time on screens whenever possible (which can be increasingly hard as so much of what we do is online) and travel much more frequently than we used to.

What's hardest about living this way?

For . . . decades, the advertising and marketing industries have been working hard to make us feel a sense of lack or insecurity. Those feelings are what make us consume the things they're selling, leading to more sales and growth for the companies they work for. The hardest part of living this way is actively choosing to reject the images of success and happiness that the media is portraying, in exchange for a life of our choosing. The difficult part is asking, "Who's ideal of living am I working towards? Why do I actually want this stuff and will it really make me feel like I want to feel?"

Once you get past that part, the rest is easy. I've met some people who don't seem to be affected by this, but it's hard to imagine with the amount of exposure we have to advertisements and ideal lifestyle imagery every day.

What's fun, rewarding, and awesome about living this way?
Just about everything is fun about living this way. I think one of the biggest misconceptions about minimalism . . . is that it's a sacrifice. One of the most unfortunate assumptions about people that choose to live simply is that they're doing it because they can't afford to do otherwise. We travel all the time because we spend less on physical possessions. We've both taken time to freelance or quit our full-time jobs and had so much more flexibility because of our choice to do this. We get to choose our own enjoyment and I can't see why anyone wouldn't want to live with only the things they actually want and little of the rest.

What advice would you give to someone who wants to create a smaller impact on Earth but isn't sure where to start?
Start donating, recycling, or throwing away one item per day. Every day you learn to make a decision about what you want in your life and what you don't. Most often, feeling overwhelmed and frustrated comes from a lack of clarity about what we actually want. As you make that small decision each day, your ability to make it will improve. When that feels comfortable, move up to two items or three items every day. It's not the stuff, but your ability to confidently make those choices and take action based on the outcome that truly empowers you to design a life of your choosing.

One approach is to have honest conversations with these folks. Explain how you feel, and say you'd like to take a break. If you can't do that—no matter the reason—start by declining invitations. Over time, most people will get the hint. If they don't, try being honest. You can also change your after-school activities to meet new people. Overall, make a goal of spending your time with the people you really love being with.

Do you feel unprepared to handle these transitions on your own? Talk to trusted friends or adults, and get their input and advice. They may have insights and suggestions that could make tough conversations easier or the ending of friendships less harsh.

Just as you want to make sure you don't regret giving things away, make sure you're truly ready to end a relationship. It's often really hard to reestablish a friendship after you've pushed someone away. But if someone often stresses you out or drags you down, part of your minimalist journey may include parting ways. Trust your intuition.

FOCUS LESS ON STUFF ... WITH FRIENDS

Possibly, your friends and peers won't understand your decision to live with less or you won't feel comfortable discussing this choice with them. You can still steer your shared activities and behaviors to be less stuff-focused. Say no to spending time at the mall in favor of bike rides or movie marathons. For celebrating birthdays and holidays,

If you don't have a yard or green space where you live, check out community gardening in your area. It's a great way to meet people and to go green.

give the gift of experiences instead of buying physical things. For example, give a friend a gift of baking cookies together or making a favorite craft together. Incorporate carpooling, recycling, thrift shopping, and other eco-conscious practices into your group activities. Suggest doing work in a shared urban garden, going on a hike, or volunteering to help pick up trash at a local park. You can do all this without ever launching into a preachy rant about global waste.

LEARN TO BE IN THE MOMENT

Minimalist choices lead to clarity, freedom, and feelings of serenity. Being kind to the planet in every way you can will help you feel like a responsible, community-minded citizen.

MINIMALIST CHALLENGE: GIFT GIVING

Minimalist gift giving can be tricky. You don't want to impose your views or life choices on someone who might not be ready to downshift into simpler living. You also don't want to seem like a cheapskate or slacker when an important birthday rolls around. Gift certificates for back rubs or plaques promising to do someone else's chores were cute when you were ten years old, but they may seem like cop-outs as you get older.

Gifting an experience instead of an object is a great way to make someone feel special, create shared memories, and reduce the number of physical items exchanged. So the next time you dream up a gift idea, think of something that won't sit on a shelf or in a closet. Here are a few suggestions to get your imagination fired up:

- Buy gift cards for the recipient's favorite movie theater, and make a date to see a matinee together.
- Schedule mani-pedis for the both of you at a nearby salon. Prepay for the services, and write a card with all the details. Or offer to exchange mani-pedis. It can be fun to do this on the back stoop on a warm day or in a cozy spot at home in the winter.
- Pay for a class or seminar, such as pottery, cooking, jewelry making, or martial arts, that you know the person will love. Check your area's community education catalog for affordable classes.
- Get tickets to a concert or theater performance that you know the recipient would enjoy.
- Offer to go to a favorite state park or hiking spot for a day of outdoor adventure. Pack or buy a lunch for the two of you to share.

- Book some time at an indoor climbing wall.
- Reserve lanes at the local bowling alley.
- Pay for a skating session at the local ice or roller rink.

What other experiences could you give as gifts to the people you love?

Minimalists do stuff instead of buying stuff! Next time you choose a gift for a friend or a family member, think about giving that person a fun, shared experience instead of more stuff.

Releasing stuff you don't need and using as little as possible—or at least less than you've been used to—will make you feel efficient, respectful, and mindful of waste. Learning to be grateful and present in individual moments of your life can help you feel more fulfilled and less reliant on physical objects for comfort or validation. It can help you manage anxiety and stress too. By staying in the moment, you are less likely to obsess as much about challenges or scary things that lie ahead.

The website Mindfulness for Teens has a series of guided meditations designed to help you tune into the moment and use your senses in deep, new ways. Similarly, many yoga practices can teach you to be more aware of yourself and your surroundings. Most gyms offer yoga classes, many towns have yoga studios, and YouTube offers lots of free yoga tutorials you can do at home. *Be Mindful Card Deck for Teens* by Gina M. Biegel contains exercises that can help you reduce stress levels, improve your focus, and cultivate self-care practices. Search your local library for resources on meditation, focus, or mindfulness until you find an author or a book that feels authentic to you. Ask your friends and family for ideas. Stress reduction and mindfulness are on many people's minds, and they may have great suggestions to share.

TAKE IT EASY

Don't forget to be patient with yourself. Committing to a life philosophy that involves changing how you shop, eat, get around, and think about life is not easy. It will take time to get used to new practices, and some circumstances will thwart your goals, if only temporarily. This journey will have bumps in the road, and those bumps will actually help you appreciate the smooth sailing in between. You are very likely to learn from the bumps and carry forward the dos and don'ts you want to remember next time.

You will not be able to be a perfect minimalist at all times. Sometimes you'll have to buy synthetic clothes or throw away food instead of composting. Sometimes you'll have to drive many miles by yourself with no chance of carpooling. Sometimes you'll look around and realize you've accumulated a bunch of new stuff you don't need.

Being a true minimalist doesn't mean berating yourself for slip-ups. It doesn't mean holding yourself to impossibly high standards. It means making informed, low-impact decisions as often as you can. Make eco-friendly, sustainability-focused, simple, clean decisions whenever possible. When it isn't, give yourself a pass. Be patient and gentle with yourself as you adjust to the new parameters you've set. After all, you want these changes to make your life feel less cluttered, less exhausting, and less toxic. Minimalism isn't just about purging your closet. It's about reframing your priorities. One of those priorities is your own happiness and well-being. Keep trying, knowing that most big changes come with committing—and recommitting—over time.

Minimal living doesn't come easily to everyone, and there's no one right way to simplify. Every minimalist lives a unique life. If a suggestion doesn't feel workable, consider your own parameters and dream up new and innovative ways to make your activities, space, and world less cluttered and more mindful.

SOURCE NOTES

28 Owen Rader, interview with the author, August 1, 2017.

46–47 Sarah Von Bargen, interview with the author, July 7, 2017.

83 "How It Works," Boomerang Bags, accessed March 12, 2018, http://boomerangbags.org/about.

90 Marie Kondo, *The Life-Changing Magic of Tidying Up: The Japanese Art of Decluttering and Organizing* (Emeryville, CA: Ten Speed, 2014), 39.

94–95 Anthony Ungaro, interview with the author, July 31, 2017.

GLOSSARY

boomerang bags: volunteer-made reusable bags created from recycled materials. Many groups make these bags and give them away as an alternative to plastic bags.

capsule wardrobe: a subset of your main wardrobe (about thirty-five pieces) that you wear for a set time as an exercise in minimalist living

climate change: an increase in temperatures on Earth caused mostly by increased levels of carbon dioxide in the atmosphere. The extra carbon dioxide comes from burning fossil fuels.

compost: decayed organic matter that is used as fertilizer. Many people make compost at home by collecting food waste in a bin.

consignment: selling items through a dealer, who pays the owner a portion of the proceeds when the goods are purchased. Many secondhand and online clothing stores sell goods on consignment.

ecosystem: a biological community of living things and the environment in which they exist. Members of an ecosystem depend on one another for survival. Examples include a forest that provides a home and food for many plants and animals.

environmentalism: a social movement that promotes conservation of resources, recycling, protecting wildlife, and other practices that help protect the natural world from human-made harms

fast fashion: designing, producing, and selling new clothing, shoes, and accessories rapidly and cheaply. Fast fashion maximizes profits for clothing brands by bringing large numbers of products to market often and very quickly, thereby increasing sales.

fertilizer: a natural or synthetic substance that provides nutrients to plants. Compost is a natural fertilizer.

fossil fuel: a fuel formed inside Earth from the remains of ancient plants or animals. Coal, petroleum, and natural gas are examples of fossil fuels.

locavore: a person whose diet consists only or mainly of locally grown or produced food

meditation: a mental exercise that involves quieting one's mind to reach a heightened level of spiritual awareness

mindfulness: a mental state achieved by focusing attention on the present moment

minimalism: a lifestyle of using less, minimizing harm to the environment, and owning only items that are useful. Minimalism in art, music, and literature focuses on spare, uncluttered works.

organic: derived from or relating to living organisms. When organic materials decay, they break down into a fertile soil called humus.

organic farming: growing crops without chemical pesticides or fertilizers. It also refers to raising livestock without antibiotics and growth hormones that make animals grow more quickly but also can be harmful to the humans who consume their meat or milk.

pesticide: a substance used to destroy insects that eat crops. Many large farms apply toxic chemical pesticides to their fields.

petroleum: a fuel formed inside Earth from the remains of ancient plants and animals. Many plastics and synthetic fibers are made from petroleum.

recycling: collecting, processing, and reusing materials instead of throwing them away. Most households in the United States recycle paper, cardboard, glass jars, metal cans, and plastic food containers. Some communities also recycle electronics. Recycling businesses process these materials and turn them into new products.

sustainability: maintainable over a long time without causing harm or disruption. Sustainable minimalistic practices don't harm people, animals, or Earth.

synthetic: a material not found naturally on Earth but that is manufactured. Examples include plastics and human-made fibers such as polyester.

thrifting: buying items secondhand at thrift stores

upcycling: repurposing old objects for new uses, such as transforming an old picture frame into an earring holder

SELECTED BIBLIOGRAPHY

Arnold, Jeanne E., Anthony P. Graesch, Enzo Ragazzini, and Elinor Ochs. *Life at Home in the Twenty-First Century: 32 Families Open Their Doors*. Los Angeles: Cotsen Institute of Archaeology Press, 2017.

Chandler, Adam. "Why Americans Lead the World in Food Waste." *Atlantic*, July 15, 2016. https://www.theatlantic.com/business/archive/2016/07/american-food-waste/491513/.

Cline, Elizabeth. "The Power of Buying Less by Buying Better." *Atlantic*, February 16, 2016. https://www.theatlantic.com/business/archive/2016/02/buying-less-by-buying-better/462639/.

Conca, James. "Making Climate Change Fashionable—the Garment Industry Takes On Global Warming." *Forbes*, December 3, 2015. https://www.forbes.com/sites/jamesconca/2015/12/03/making-climate-change-fashionable-the-garment-industry-takes-on-global-warming/#4d93066a79e4.

Haspel, Tamar. "Is Organic Agriculture Really Better for the Environment?" *Washington Post*, May 14, 2016. https://www.washingtonpost.com/lifestyle/food/is-organic-agriculture-really-better-for-the-environment/2016/05/14/e9996dce-17be-11e6-924d-838753295f9a_story.html?utm_term=.82a3ea60ea11.

Jacobs, Harrison. "Why Grocery Stores Like Trader Joe's Throw Out So Much Perfectly Good Food." Business Insider, October 15, 2014. http://www.businessinsider.com/why-grocery-stores-throw-out-so-much-food-2014-10.

Lovell, Sophie. *Dieter Rams: As Little Design as Possible*. London: Phaidon, 2011.

Merrick, Amy. "Why Students Aren't Fighting Forever 21." *New Yorker*, June 6, 2014. https://www.newyorker.com/business/currency/why-students-arent-fighting-forever-21.

Millburn, Joshua Fields, and Ryan Nicodemus. *Minimalism: Live a Meaningful Life*. Missoula, MT: Asymmetrical, 2011.

Rosenberg, David. "What Life Was Like in Taylor Camp, Hawaii's Legendary Hippie Haven." *Slate*, August 2, 2015. http://www.slate.com/blogs/behold/2015/08/02/john_wehrheim_s_taylor_camp_a_look_at_an_alternative_community_in_kauai.html.

Simmons, Ann M. "The World's Trash Crisis, and Why Many Americans Are Oblivious." *Los Angeles Times*, April 22, 2016. http://beta.latimes .com/world/global-development/la-fg-global-trash-20160422-20160421 -snap-htmlstory.html.

Spivack, Emily. "Wartime Rationing and Nylon Riots." Smithsonian.com, September 4, 2012. https://www.smithsonianmag.com/arts-culture /stocking-series-part-1-wartime-rationing-and-nylon-riots-25391066/.

Strasser, Susan. *Waste and Want: A Social History of Trash*. New York: Metropolitan Books, 1999.

Timm, Jane C. "Millennials: We Care More about the Environment." *MSNBC*, March 22, 2014. http://www.msnbc.com/morning-joe /millennials-environment-climate-change.

Waxman, Olivia. "The History of Recycling Is More Complicated Than You May Think." *Time*, November 15, 2016. http://time.com/4568234 /history-origins-recycling/.

Wicker, Alden. "Fast Fashion Is Creating an Environmental Crisis." *Newsweek*, September 1, 2016. http://www.newsweek.com/2016 /09/09/old-clothes-fashion-waste-crisis-494824.html.

FURTHER INFORMATION

Books

Becker, Joshua. *The More of Less: Finding the Life You Want under Everything You Own*. Colorado Springs, CO: WaterBrook, 2016.
Teens and adults alike have praised this book for being practical, supportive, and nonjudgmental. Becker is also the mind behind the blog *Becoming Minimalist*. This book is his guide to customizing a life with less to suit your needs.

Bloom, Jonathan. *American Wasteland: How America Throws Away Nearly Half of Its Food (and What We Can Do about It)*. Cambridge, MA: Lifelong Books, 2011.
This award-winning exposé on American food waste is bound to inspire some grocery-related habit changes.

Cline, Elizabeth L. *Overdressed: The Shockingly High Cost of Cheap Fashion*. New York: Portfolio, 2012.
Cline provides a thorough and eye-opening exploration of how and why fast fashion is a destructive industry.

Cornell, Kari, and Jenny Larson. *The Craft-a-Day Book: 30 Projects to Make with Recycled Materials*. Minneapolis: Twenty-First Century Books, 2018.
The author-photographer team presents thirty upcycling projects to make from items around the house or from thrift stores. Beginners and experienced crafters will find the right project in this book.

Donovan, Sandy. *Thrift Shopping: Discovering Bargains and Hidden Treasures*. Minneapolis: Twenty-First Century Books, 2015.
Looking for the right outfit for a big party? Or maybe you want some funky shelves for your bedroom. Instead of heading for the mall, check out a thrift store. This book discusses how to save money and help the planet by buying secondhand.

Gunders, Dana. *Waste-Free Kitchen Handbook: A Guide to Eating Well and Saving Money by Wasting Less Food*. San Francisco: Chronicle Books, 2015.
Written by a senior scientist at the Natural Resources Defense Council, this book aims to help people waste less and use more food.

Hughes, Meredith Sayes. *Plants vs. Meats: The Health, History, and Ethics of What We Eat*. Minneapolis: Twenty-First Century Books, 2016.
This book explores the cultural history of food and examines debates about nutrition, agriculture, and food distribution in modern times. It's a great book to help readers make decisions about how and what they choose to eat.

Kallen, Stuart A. *Trashing the Planet: Examining Our Global Garbage Glut.*
    Minneapolis: Twenty-First Century Books, 2018.
    Humans have polluted the air, the oceans, and even outer space. This
    book examines the global garbage crisis and explores efforts to clean up
    the mess.

Kondo, Marie. *The Life-Changing Magic of Tidying Up: The Japanese Art of
    Decluttering and Organizing.* Emeryville, CA: Ten Speed, 2014.
    A best seller for many years, Kondo's book focuses on minimalism and
    decluttering as paths to inner peace.

Seo, Danny. *Upcycling: Create Beautiful Things with the Stuff You Already
    Have.* Philadelphia: Running Press, 2011.
    This book helps people transform old, worn-out stuff into cool, upcycled
    objects. It includes tutorials on turning wine corks into bathmats, old
    scarves into blankets, tote bags into floor cushions, and dozens of other
    projects.

Vo, Dzung X. *The Mindful Teen: Powerful Skills to Help You Handle Stress
    One Moment at a Time.* Oakland: Instant Help Books, 2015.
    Focused on reducing teen stress, this book offers an easy-to-apply
    mindfulness program to help you manage stress in healthy ways,
    improve communication, and reduce conflicts with family and friends.

Websites

Becoming Minimalist
    http://www.becomingminimalist.com
    Minimalist author Joshua Becker runs this site, a collection of posts
    designed to help all readers tap their inner minimalists. The focus is on
    living with less as a route to serenity and happiness.

Boomerang Bags
    http://boomerangbags.org
    Launched in Australia, this movement has branches around the world,
    including the United States. Join or start a group in your neighborhood
    and become part of the effort to make reusable tote bags from donated
    fabrics.

Break the Twitch
https://www.breakthetwitch.com/
A popular blog by recovering maximalist Anthony Ongaro, this site gives advice on simplifying everything from meals, morning routines, and wardrobes to musings on how to be a minimalist in ways that personally suit you.

Composting Is Way Easier Than You Think
Natural Resources Defense Council
https://www.nrdc.org/stories/composting-way-easier-you-think?gclid=CO6H8_Oi9dQCFYeFswodZgoBdQ
This article offers simple tips on how to create an effective, stink-free, Earth-friendly compost setup virtually anywhere.

Goodnet
https://www.goodnet.org
You'll find dozens of how-to articles on this site designed to help you help the world. The post titled "7 Ways to Donate Second Hand Goods" (http://www.goodnet.org/articles/543) includes advice on getting rid of old bikes, cell phones, books, and more.

Grechen's Closet
http://grechenscloset.com
Grechen Rubin is a longtime fashion blogger and self-confessed shopaholic who has written extensively about her desire to become a minimalist. Her posts will resonate with fashionistas who long to do right by the planet but also adore buying and wearing the latest trends.

Greener Living
https://www.epa.gov/environmental-topics/greener-living
Part of the EPA website, Greener Living includes practical advice on reducing your environmental footprint.

Minimalism
http://www.theartstory.org/movement-minimalism.htm
This site is devoted to the history of minimalism in art. It focuses on minimalist artists of the 1960s but also explores the roots of minimalism from earlier in the twentieth century.

Sadie Seasongoods
http://www.sadieseasongoods.com
Going strong since 2013, this repurposing and upcycling blog is packed with inspiration and ideas. Find ways to reuse everyday items for home decor and fashion projects.

Sustainable America
http://www.sustainableamerica.org
This website and blog focuses mainly on food waste and how to avoid it. It delves into other sustainability topics too. The "Resources" page provides access to infographics, research papers, and videos on food and fuel waste.

Zen Habits
https://zenhabits.net
This blog includes many posts on minimalism, focusing mainly on mindfulness, gratitude, and inner peace. It's a great resource for people hoping to simplify their lives from the inside out.

Online Films

Food Inc.
http://www.pbs.org/pov/foodinc
This film from the Public Broadcasting System (PBS) explores the increasingly mechanized farms in the United States and discusses how their practices impact human health and the environment.

Thrive with Less
http://thrivewithless.com
Follow six student filmmakers at Michigan State University as they complete six minimalist challenges over one month and do their best to strip away all excess from their lives.

The True Cost
https://truecostmovie.com
This documentary produced by Life Is My Movie Entertainment explores the catastrophic impact of fast fashion on the environment, farmers, and textile workers.

INDEX

ABOUT THE AUTHOR

Sally McGraw is a Minneapolis-based freelance writer, editor, and ghostwriter. She holds a creative writing degree from Binghamton University and spent ten years working in the book and magazine publishing industry before striking out on her own in 2011. She is the creator of popular style and body image blog *Already Pretty* (alreadypretty.com) and the author of several books for teens, including *Find Your Style: Boost Your Body Image through Fashion Confidence*. In her free time, McGraw mentors emerging women leaders, studies Tae Kwon Do, scours eBay for secondhand fashion finds, and attempts to entertain her two kooky cats.

PHOTO ACKNOWLEDGMENTS

Image credits: Mariabo2015/Shutterstock.com, p. 1 (plant); graphixmania/Shutterstock.com, p. 1 (T-shirt); VoodooDot/Shutterstock.com, p. 1; (bike) Preappy/Moment/Getty Images, p. 4; Tim Clark/Alamy Stock Photo, p. 6; Ann Ronan Pictures/Print Collecto/Getty Images, p. 8; Universal History Archiv/Getty Images, p. 10; Library of Congress (LC-USZC2-5676), p. 13; State Archives of Florida/Florida Memory/Alamy Stock Photo, p. 14; UIG/Getty Images, p. 17; Cn0ra/iStock/Getty Images, p. 19; Kathy deWitt/Alamy Stock Photo, p. 20; Zakir Chowdhury/Barcroft Images/Getty Images, p. 24; Roy James Shakespeare All Rights Reserve/Getty Images, p. 26; MUNIR UZ ZAMAN/AFP/Getty Images, p. 30; rootstocks/iStock/Getty Images, p. 33; Mitchell Funk/Photographer's Choice/Getty Images, p. 36; Janine Wiedel/Getty Images, p. 38; SIMON MAINA/AFP/Getty Images, p. 40; keith morris/Alamy Stock Photo, p. 45; Uriel Sinai/Stringer/Getty Images, p. 48; Zurijeta/Shutterstock.com, p. 50; Juanmonino/E+/Getty Images, p. 52; Ryan McVay/Photodisc/Getty Images, p. 53; monkeybusinessimages/iStock/Getty Images, p. 56; Smith Collection/Iconica/Getty Images, p. 62; Education Images/UIG/Getty Images, p. 64; Todd Strand/Independent Picture Service, pp. 68, 69; imaginima/E+/Getty Images, p. 71; Heinz Tschanz-Hofmann/EyeEm/Getty Images, p. 74; Matheisl/Moment Mobile/Getty Images, p. 78; Vivian Chen/Alamy Stock Photo, p. 81; Creator/Independent Picture Service, p. 83; 2015 Kenneth C. Zirkel/Getty Images, p. 84; Martin Bond/Alamy Stock Photo, p. 85; Charles Maraia/The Image Bank/Getty Images, p. 89; AP Photo/Ten Speed Press, p. 91; skynesher/Serbia/Getty Images, p. 92; Hero Images/Getty Images, p. 97; Steve Debenport/E+/Getty Images, p. 99.

Cover: Mariabo2015/Shutterstock.com; graphixmania/Shutterstock.com; VoodooDot/Shutterstock.com.